MORE MEMOR...
OF
BOLTON

TRUE NORTH BOOKS
DEAN CLOUGH
HALIFAX
WEST YORKSHIRE
HX3 5AX
TEL 01422 344344

MORE MEMORIES OF BOLTON

THE PUBLISHERS WOULD LIKE TO THANK THE
FOLLOWING COMPANIES FOR SUPPORTING THE
PRODUCTION OF THIS BOOK

MAIN SPONSOR

BOLTON SCHOOL

BELDAM CROSSLEY LIMITED

BELLHOUSE HARTWELL & COMPANY LIMITED

BOLTON HOSPITAL SATURDAY FUND

JAMES BOOTH (BOLTON) LIMITED

BRITISH TURNTABLE COMPANY LIMITED

DUVAL SECURITIES

THE GATES SHOPPING CENTRE

HALBRO SPORTSEAR LIMITED

LAST DROP VILLAGE HOTEL

MATRA BAE DYNAMICS

PRESTONS LIMITED

RED BRIDGE INTERNATIONAL LIMITED

THISTLETHWAITE & COMPANY LIMITED

First published in Great Britain by True North Holdings
Dean Clough
Halifax HX3 5AX
1998

© TRUE NORTH HOLDINGS

ISBN 1 900 463 13 X

Introduction

The publication of our first book, *Memories of Bolton,* met with a tremendous response from the people in the town. Thousands of copies of the original book have been sold to date, with many finding their way overseas to bring pleasure to former Bolton residents who had emigrated. The letters of encouragement and kind comments we received urged us to produce a second book, this time containing even more of the excellent photographs which had provided such enjoyment. The compilation of *More Memories of Bolton* has been carried out over a period of several months. We always expected it to be a pleasurable experience, but in the event the satisfaction we have derived from studying the marvellous old photographs went far beyond our expectations.

Victoria Square in the 1950s

Increasingly, *nostalgia* is enjoyed by a growing band of people and the book is intended to appeal to a wide audience. Where possible we have tried to concentrate upon a period within the memory of most of our readers; the 1950s, 60s and 70s - decades which saw tremendous changes in the town, and a time when changes in the world of work, entertainment, public health and retailing. *Change* takes place constantly in every town and Bolton is no exception. As we all get older it is often easier to 'step back' and view events and developments with a clearer sense of perspective. Our aim has been to assist in this respect by presenting a 'catalyst' capable of rekindling memories of days gone by in an entertaining manner.

Looking through the pages of this book it may be surprising how much change has taken place, and over such a relatively short period, relative to the long history of the area. Several of Bolton's best known and longest established firms have allowed us access to their often extensive internal archives. This has enabled us to recount the history of these companies, from humble beginnings to, in most cases, leading positions in their chosen area of expertise. Of course, these organisations have tremendous social, as well as commercial significance, as between them they represent the places of employment for thousand upon thousand Bolton people. We are grateful for the co-operation and support of the directors of these businesses for adding to the quality and interest of this book.

Many of the children featured in these photographs will be reaching retirement age now and we would be pleased to hear from anyone who may have recognised themselves.

Street scenes are not neglected. Photographs of this nature were popular in the last book, and understandably so. The changing face of the town is reflected in the way our roads and shops have developed to meet the changing needs of our lives over the years. These photographs show the shops and motorcars we remember from our early days, along with the fashions which were all the rage when we were younger. All combine to refresh our memories of days gone by, and when that occurs the book will have achieved its aim.

We hope that you enjoy reading *More Memories of Bolton* as much as we enjoyed creating it.

TEXT	PETER THOMAS
COVER DESIGN/PHOTOGRAPH COMPILATION	MARK SMITH
DESIGNERS	MANDY WALKER AND NICKY BRIGHTON
BUSINESS DEVELOPMENT EDITOR	ALAN EASTHAM
COPYWRITER	SARAH PARKS

CONTENTS

Around the town centre

Were it not for the vehicles, this could look for all the world like the murky back streets of Dickensian London. However, this is very definitely Bolton and a 1940s view of Old Hall Street North from Ridgway Gates. The Old Hall was Bolton's first poor house, built in 1785. By 1812 it had become the headquarters of a kind of Bolton vigilante association - a group of citizens, under Colonel Ralph Fletcher, who took it upon themselves to keep law and order. By 1820 the Old Hall had become the Three Arrows Inn, which was demolished in 1865 to make way for the Town Hall. The shop to the right of the two cars belonged to Edward Crook, fish and game dealer since the 1930s. The interesting half-timbered style was created in 1907 to match Whitakers' new Tudor style building of that date. The building on the extreme left was the Westminster and Paris Bank, but it had previously housed the Silver Vat pub, formerly the Four Horseshoes. A more useful piece of information might be that Old Hall Street North boasts what are probably the last 'ladies only' public toilets in Lancashire - and free at that.

The vehicles give this picture a very 1950s feel, not least the Morris Minor forging up the centre of the road towards the camera. In fact, this is a 1954 view of Bradshawgate and in one respect it differs little from what might be seen now, over forty years on, Prestons the Jewellers, 'The Diamond Centre of the North', still occupies its prominent position on Deansgate. The golden ball on top of the clock tower is a 'time ball'. This was installed in 1914 and daily, at a signal from Greenwich, the ball descended to a position which indicated to local people that it was 10am. The fondness of Bolton people for the good things in life may explain the fact that Yates' Wine Lodge has now expanded to occupy the premises which, in 1954, housed Eagle Star Insurance and the Burnley Building Society. One feature which is not present now is the small tower and cupola on top of the Prince William Hotel to the right. These were removed in 1971. Perhaps the most evocative part of this photograph is the Lanry advertisement on the back of the bus. You almost get an instant whiff of that once common household bleach.

Bolton Evening News

Above: Just as anything new or abnormal in the streets of Bolton during the conflict of 1939-45 was dismissed as 'summat to do with the war', so any unusual activity in May 1953 was explained away as 'summat to do with the Coronation'. The sight of workmen installing giant tubes around the Town Hall excited all manner of specu-lation, but the explanation was quite mundane. The tubes were fluorescent light fittings to provide some illumination around the Town Hall at night. Although there may have been a wish to get them up in time for the Coronation on June 2nd, the lights were intended to have a longer lifetime than the celebrations. The workers' platform gave them an unrivalled view of both the Town Hall tower and the elaborate carvings on the pediment below. The original Town Hall was built between 1867 and 1873. Perhaps surprisingly, there was much debate about whether to have a clock tower at all because of the 'outrageous' cost of around £7000. The carved figures on the pediment represent Bolton and the sources of her cotton based nineteenth century industrial prosperity. The pediment is still there to marvel at, but the fluorescent lights are now gone.

Bolton Evening News

Above: This unusual appearance outside the Lido in August 1942 must have caused a few eyebrows to be raised. However, this was wartime, when it was usual to see the unusual. This surface water pipe along Bradshawgate was the first supply line for water from the canal and others were planned. Should the mains be damaged in an air-raid, these surface pipes were to act as an emergency water supply for the fire-fighting services. Such features were a normal sight in many towns and cities, for the German 'Blitz' of 1940-1 had produced harrowing scenes of fires raging uncontrollably while water fountained away out of damaged mains. Bolton itself had escaped relatively unscathed by 1942, although bombs which fell on Ardwick Street and Punch Street in October 1941 had claimed 11 lives. However, nobody could foretell the future. Fortunately the terrifying V1 and V2 attacks of 1944 came too late in the war to make a lot of difference. The V1 flying bombs, or 'doodlebugs', along with the V2 rockets, caused widespread fear and hundreds of children were evacuated to Bolton from London. However, the 'doodlebugs' which fell on nearby Radcliffe, Tottington and Worsley, on Christmas Eve 1944, showed that nobody was really safe.

Facing page, top: The elegantly dressed lady may be contemplating catching a train to Southport, as advertised at Trinity Street station in 1936. On the other hand she may be waiting for a taxi or a tram as this was both the tram terminus and the taxi cab approach. What the picture does not make clear is that this was a railway bridge which had been widened in the 1890s to accommodate the cab approach at this side, along with the new booking hall and parcels office opposite. The sight of that wonderful old vehicle nosing forward may make tram enthusiasts drool, but within three years many of them had been scrapped and replaced by buses. As a bus terminus, however, the bridge was increasingly carrying much more weight than it was built for. In 1968 work began on completely replacing the bridge and the canopy shown on the 1936 picture was dismantled. The bakery referred to was the Lancashire Cash Bakery Co, in Lever Street. The rest of the station buildings were demolished in 1987 and new booking offices were opened on the opposite side of the street. As a nice touch in conservation, however, the clock tower was spared and incorporated into the new building.

Bottom: Judging by dress and vehicles, this view of Bradshawgate dates from the late 1940s. The nationally well-known name of Prudential can be seen on the left. Opposite, the bowl of a pipe is just visible to advertise the wares of Arthur Morris, a locally famous tobacconist's shop which still trades at this spot along Bradshawgate.

At the first junction to the left is Nelson Square. The fine and imposing building on the corner, with the triangular pediment over the door, is the Pack Horse. This hotel was built in 1904 and is a reminder of how public and commercial buildings around this time were built with a symmetry and style which is pleasing to the eye.

Many modern day structures seem bland and uniform in comparison. Opposite the doorway of the Pack Horse is the statue of Samuel Crompton, Bolton's most famous 'son'. It was in Hall-i'th'-Wood, Tonge, that Crompton invented the spinning 'mule' in 1779, an invention which truly revolutionised the spinning process. The 'mule' enabled spinning to become factory based and much of the future prosperity of Bolton and Lancashire rested on Crompton's work. Unfortunately, Crompton died in poverty and debt in 1827.

Below: A wet December day in 1955 has not deterred the shoppers in Newport Street in this shot which has the Town Hall clock as its background. It should have been a good time of year for the Raincoat Company, whose premises can be seen on the far left. If any more evidence of the season is required, the back of the No 23 bus provides it. 'Buy Wintergrade Esso' is the rather chilly message.

The invitation to 'Buy UCP Tripe' on the building immediately in front of the bus is one which most people would find eminently resistible today. However, in the less prosperous 1950s, a visit to the tripe shop was a regular feature in the lives of most working-class households. It offered a cheaper meal than even the fish and chip shop.

For those whose memories go back so far, tripe slipped down the throat quite easily, although it tasted of little else than the condiments you put on it. The other delicacies from the tripe shop were cowheel and elder. The former was very chewy, whilst the latter had a thick, clogging consistency. In all cases, it was not wise to think too much about which parts of the animal you were eating!

Right: Newport Street in the 1950s was a lively little commercial area with a good range of shops. The view is from Great Moor Street towards Victoria Square and the Town Hall. A little cluster of people have congregated outside the 'Brighter Homes' wallpaper shop and there is no doubt that the prams are far more impressive than the cars further down the street. These formidable 'coachbuilt' prams were a feature of the time - large, well sprung and very expensive. Hesford's jewellers can be seen and next to that, on the corner, is Kettering's shoe shop. Battersby's Furniture Showrooms are presenting a bold front and next to these is the butcher's shop of Boardman's. The white building towards the end of Newport Street, just beyond the van, is the Grey Mare public house. These premises are always supposed to have been built to publish the 'Bolton Chronicle' in 1824. Some of the upper storeys at this end of the street look distinctly worn and all the property on view along Newport Street was demolished between 1957 and 1958. A row of flat-roofed modern shops was built and traffic islands were introduced. A major change came yet again, in 1969, with the pedestrianisation of the area.

An incredible choice of entertainment and intoxicating beverages could be enjoyed by anyone visiting Churchgate in 1947/48. This photograph contains two theatres, one cinema, two temperance bars and seven public houses. Just visible to the right is the lamp of The Man and Scythe, the oldest inn in Bolton, reputedly built in 1251. A very strong locally held belief is that James, the seventh Earl of Derby, spent his last hours there before his execution at the Market Cross in October 1651. This penalty was imposed for his part in the Royalist attack on Bolton in 1644 and the subsequent 'Bolton Massacre'. The Manor of Bolton belonged to the Derby family at various times over a period of 700 years and this connection is emphasised in the name of the Derby Arms Hotel, further down Churchgate. Across the road the Golden Lion, later a Berni Inn, reverted to its nickname the Brass Cat, in 1995.

The Capitol Cinema, on the left, opened in 1929 and its fine frontage is typical of the time. The Grand Theatre and the Theatre Royal were also to be found along Churchgate and the canopy of the latter can be seen, just before the Derby Arms.

Above: The 'art deco' 1930s frontage of the Lido Cinema and the older style architecture of the King's Hall make an interesting contrast in this 1950s photograph. The 'golden age' of the cinema began in the 1920s, with the advent of the 'talkies'. Moving films had the power to evoke distant, more glamorous worlds and the names of early cinemas often hinted at the strange and the exotic. The Rialto, the Palladium, the Tivoli - all have slightly more allure than the rather prosaic ABC or Showcase. The Lido, on Bradshawgate, had a name very much in the romantic tradition. It opened on March 27th 1937 and its internal decorative scheme included scenes of Venice. The opening night included operatic singing; also classical dance accompanied by Reginald Liversedge on the Christie organ. Then came the feature film, 'Evergreen', starring Jessie Matthews. Over the course of 60 years the Lido remained as a cinema which also hosted stage shows. For a time, in the early 60s, it was given over entirely to Bingo, but after a £4000 'facelift' the Lido had a triumphant return to films in 1964. The cinema later became part of the ABC group until its very recent closure.

Right: 'Bark St Mill for Bargains' is proclaimed proudly on the old Flax Mill chimney and indeed Bridge Street seems to be awash with bargains in this shot of 1936. 'Nothing Over 6d' is another eye-catcher, this time to the right. This, of course, was the Woolworth motto for many years. The very distinctive cupola topped tower, at the far end of Bridge Street, represented adver-tising in another form, for all locals would have recognised this as the Co-operative Drapery Store - reasonable prices guaranteed. Sadly, there were no more bargains to be had at the old fish market, which had been demolished in 1932/33. It had been sited just to the left of where the tram is pulling away - in itself a wonderfully evocative sight. The Imperial Playhouse, in the foreground, had only 11 years of life left, but in 1936 it was going strong with 'She Shall Have Music', featuring Jack Hilton and his band.

The view is a greatly changed one today and although the Flax Mill chimney was preserved in the changes of the 1960s, it was later demolished to make way for the Bark Street redevelopment scheme.

Bolton Evening News

Above: A sad story of closed pubs is one theme of this early 1960s view of Churchgate looking towards the tall tower of the Parish Church. The two public houses on the right both had a Derby connection. The Cornbrook Ales sign belonged to the Derby Arms. The link of the Legs of Man Hotel with the Derby family was that historically the family provided governors to the Isle of Man. The entire block of buildings was demolished in the 1960s to make way for new office blocks, including the one which houses the 'Bolton Evening News'. Pubs had clearly become an endangered species at this end of Churchgate, although the Boar's Head, to the left, hung on until 1992. It was demolished in 1997, but is soon to be rebuilt. The low white building nearest the camera on the left, is Walsh's famous Pastie Shop, still going strong today. This building has been in existence since at least 1667 and parts of the interior are considerably older. Just beyond the Boar's Head was Church House Garage. This contained a huge turntable for cars which came in for petrol. The varied traffic on Churchgate includes an increasingly rare sight by the 1960s - a horse and cart.

Above right: A Volkswagen 'Beetle' shares 'pole' position as the cars impatiently wait at the traffic lights. You can almost feel feet twitching over accelerators and eyes fixed on red lights, waiting for that first hint of amber. This shot of Bradshawgate in December 1971, looking north from the Queen's Cinema corner, has a car dominated theme, although a couple of

buses lurk in the distance. There was much to catch the eye at Parker's Motor Factors, which no longer exists on this site. In 1971, however, it was quite a substantial concern, offering the usual range of accessories and spares, along with cars themselves. Although the general scenario is quite up-to-date, it is the publicity material in Parker's showroom window which gives the feel of times past. 'British Press Acclaim Avenger. Demonstrations Arranged'. How long ago that now seems - a time when the Hillman Avenger was a new model! Many of the buildings beyond Parker's have also changed their function since 1971, including the Queen's Hotel, the Brown Cow public house and the Bolton Corporation Transport Offices. The first bright sign on the left-hand side belonged to the Clarence Hotel, now also gone.

On a chilly December evening in 1971, the bright lights of Bradshawgate illuminate a problem that was only going to get worse. The growth of car ownership has been one of the most liberating developments of the century. Access to a motor-car has allowed more choice in terms of work, shopping, leisure and holidays for ordinary working people. At certain times of the day, however, in urban centres the 'downside' of all this can become apparent - traffic congestion, frustration, unhealthy fumes. The number of people present in this photograph, which was taken from Preston's Jewellers, suggests the early evening rush hour. A similar shot today would undoubtedly show an even more traffic congested Bradshawgate. The first shop on the right in the 1971 scene is Lennards. A little further down, the pub sign belongs to the Fleece. This was built on the site of the Old Fleece Inn, which had been demolished in a road-widening project of 1907. In 1972 the Fleece was to become the Gaiety and in 1983, with the addition of two shops, Maxim's. Just down from the Fleece, the lights shine outside Yates' Wine Lodge which has occupied this building from 1906 to the present-day.

Below: It looks a long way across Knowsley Street to these ladies at the traffic lights and some of them are none too sure about it. There were no such aids as 'little green men' in 1963 and crossing at a busy junction needed perfect timing. There are one or two vehicles on view that are very '1960s'. The A40 Farina turning to the right is one of these, as is the scooter, much beloved by the 1960s 'mods'. The buildings on the right are of much interest. The solid and substantial Knowsley House accommodated such well-known retailers as John Collier, tailors and Dr Scholl, footwear specialists, as well as offices above. Just beyond Knowsley House and across Corporation Street was Stokes' Opticians, a business which remains today. The Market Hall is clearly visible, but the camera angle does not do justice to its magnificent Classical entrance. First opened in 1855, it was refurbished as a showpiece Victorian Market Hall in the 1980s. Readers might like to test their powers of recall by considering the following names which could be found further along Knowsley Street in 1963 - 'Pot' Baileys, Percivals, Proffit's Slot TV.

Below: There is a nice contrast of architectural styles in this photograph of Great Moor Street in 1963. A block of new shops displays the hallmarks of much of the building done in the 1960s - bland, functional and cheap. No doubt this was born out of financial constraints and these shoppers are probably looking for value for money rather than an aesthetic experience. Nevertheless, nobody would feel inclined to stand for long and let his or her eye rove over this soulless structure. The buildings around have got more to offer , although there is only a tantalising glimpse of the promising looking Wheatsheaf Hotel to the right, separated from the shops by Coronation Street. In the background, at a right-angle to the shops, stands Howell Croft South. These houses present a good contrast in style to the shops and the name has historical connections. Howell Croft was named after the prominent Howell family, who owned the croft or meadow on which the houses were built. A road existed from at least 1791, ending in the meadows where the Town Hall was later built. The Flag Hotel can be seen at the far left of Howell Croft. The Flag was closed in 1970 and demolished in 1971.

Bottom: A fine day in July 1957 finds Victoria Square basking in sunshine. Shoppers stroll around whilst others simply take it easy on the benches. Victoria Square has had a chequered career. The earlier part of the nineteenth century saw it almost as an oasis, with an orchard and a meadow containing a small stream. By around 1824, however, it had become the new Market Place as the old market area in Churchgate was considered to be too congested. In the twentieth century, the Square became the principal terminus for Bolton's buses until Moor Lane was utilised for this purpose from 1930. The erecting of the War Memorial, seen on the left of the photograph, also had something to do with the decision. The Memorial was unveiled by the Earl of Derby in July 1928 and it was considered inappropriate for buses to be 'jostling' around in an area that deserved a more contemplative atmosphere. The fine and substantial building at the far end, the Commercial Hotel, was still a popular 'watering hole' in 1957, but it was closed and demolished in 1972. Victoria Square is now better known as 'The Precinct', with shopping and strolling a good deal easier in this pedestrianised area.

At leisure

'The Mecca of all the town at holiday times'. This was the description of the 78 acres of Moss Bank Park by a local writer in the 1930s and this group of visitors are finding plenty to admire in the Rockery. The picture dates from 1937, the Park itself having been opened in June 1928. Moss Bank House had been the centre of a large bleaching concern in the hands of the Ainsworth Family. The business at the 'Moss' no longer existed when the council purchased the entire estate on the death of Colonel Ainsworth. At the opening ceremony of Moss Bank Park the Mayor, Alderman Cheadle, stressed 'the value of parks as an aid to public health'. This was the key to it all - open spaces and fresh air, especially at weekends, for Boltonians who might have spent all week amidst the noise and confinement of mill work. All classes, however, flocked to Moss Bank Park and the photograph reveals a good social cross-section. The Rockery opened in 1932 with a variety of Alpine and English plants.

Shrubs and terraced walks provided a tranquil setting for the fish pond, which is the centre of attraction for the visitors in the photograph.

Bolton Evening News

Both pictures: In the later nineteenth century, Victorian town and city planners came to regard parks as the 'lungs' of urban areas. This was particularly true of industrial towns where the fumes from hundreds of factory chimneys, combined with the smoke from domestic chimney pots, darkened the skies and polluted the atmosphere. Seen in this light, then, the aerial shot of Queen's Park in 1935 shows one of Bolton's most important 'lungs'. Queen's Park was opened with all due ceremony on May 24th 1866. There was a grand procession and the singing of the 'Old Hundredth' hymn. The 56 acre park had a formal lay-out of ornamental flower beds and rose gardens which are clearly visible on the photograph. Around these can also be seen the rolling green spaces interspersed by trees. Other facilities included bowling and putting greens, tennis

courts, a paddling pool and a bandstand. Changes have taken place over the years. In 1952, for example, a new conservatory housing exotic plants was opened, the gift of Mr M W Wigglesworth. However, Queen's Park from the air in 1998 would not look a lot different from the way it did in 1935.

If Queen's Park represented the dreams of the planners in 1866, dreams of a quite different kind are the theme of this superb action shot taken in Queen's Park almost 100 years later. The formality of the rose gardens gives way to the spontaneity and joy of a game of football. The date of the photograph was probably sometime in the 1950s and the key piece of evidence is the snake belt around the waist of our highest flying footballer. Many men will remember that useful little 'hook on' elasticated belt, which seemed quite stylish at the time. The mundane background to the picture may only be a gasholder and two old men as spectators, but as the ball soars in the air Queen's Park could be Burnden Park for these boys. Just for a few moments they can dream that they are playing alongside their heroes - Lofthouse, Parry, Holden - with the roar of thousands of spectators in their ears. Nowadays the power of television and money have transformed football to such a degree that boys in any town are likely to be sporting the shirts of the most fashionable clubs. In the 1950s there was only one club for Bolton boys - the Wanderers.

Both pictures: Cheery smiles from the donkey riders and if they shut their eyes they can imagine that they are on Blackpool sands. This scene was captured in July 1952, in the middle of the Bolton holiday fortnight. Not everyone went away during Wakes weeks and for the stay-at-homes the attractions of Moss Bank Park acted like a magnet. Thousands flocked there to enjoy the swings and roundabouts, as well as that perennial children's favourite, the Punch and Judy Show. The donkey rides, provided for many years by the Court family, were a bit special. Quite a few Boltonians will remember their jingling bells and decorated harnesses. The youngsters in this photograph are about to experience that sensation of holding tight and hoping for the best. Not quite the Big Dipper - but a thrill all the same. The thick coats on display make it all too clear that this was 'typical' Wakes Weeks weather. People in Bolton could only console themselves by thinking that they would have been no better off in Blackpool.

What a contrast is provided by this scene of the following year, which shows Moss Bank Park basking in a September heatwave. The ladies and girls are making the most of what might be their last chance to wear those summer dresses before Autumn sets in. No doubt the ice-creams and swings were in great demand as far as the youngsters were concerned. For the adults, perhaps it was enough just to sit and soak up the late afternoon sun. Not that this was all that Moss Bank had to offer. Its rolling 78 acres provided opportunities for tennis, bowling and putting and there were regular band concerts. Since the opening of the Park in 1928, there had been a constant development of its attractions. The famous Rockery and fish pond had opened in 1932, with terraced paths winding their way through Alpine and English plants and shrubs. In 1947 the 'Old English Garden' had been established. This secluded, walled area was soon attracting crowds of visitors to admire the profusion of flowers. Only one month before the September heatwave featured in the photograph, a new Open Air Theatre seating 2000, the generous gift of Mr J W Wigglesworth, had been opened. It staged a Coronation pageant later in August.

Bolton Evening News

Both pictures: Bolton Holiday Week is the theme linking these two photographs of Moor Lane Bus Station taken in 1947 and 1948. At this time it was customary for Lancashire and Yorkshire mills to grind to a halt for one week (later a fortnight) every summer, whilst the whole town took a holiday. The towns took it in turn to 'shut up shop' and Bolton's week traditionally fell at the end of June. This 1947 photograph of Moor Lane captures the holiday mood. Perhaps it was innate pessimism, or perhaps locks really were more fragile in those days, but there was always someone with a bulging suitcase roped up around the middle. The July 1948 photograph captures Moor Lane at a quieter time of day but the local newspaper recorded 40 Ribble coaches leaving for day-trips on July 1st 1948, as well as service and duplicate buses leaving every five minutes for the popular resorts. These included Blackpool, Morecambe, Rhyl, Windermere and Harrogate. It was estimated that over 5000 holiday-makers would be returning from Blackpool the following weekend, along with 2000 or so from Morecambe. By the Thursday of holiday week, Bolton Central Post Office had handled 55,070 postcards and 1270 parcels, many of the latter containing kippers from the Isle of Man. The 'Bolton Evening News' recorded all of the 'ins and outs' of Boltonians on holiday despite the fact that the editor himself, Frank Singleton, was on holiday in the Isle of Man, where he gave a lecture to the Douglas Rotary Club with the awe-inspiring title of 'Spare Time Novel Writing'.

The Bolton Holiday Week of 1948 was cold and dull, but these things were taken stoically and for most people it was back to work the following Monday. There would be plenty of tales to tell, especially about 'digs' and seaside landladies. What a formidable breed they were at this time, with their rules and regulations on every dark corner of the stairs - 'Strictly no food or drink permitted in rooms', or 'Visitors must vacate the establishment between meals'. Out you had to go, even if 'earthquake, wind and fire' raged along the promenade.

So much is different today from 1948. Now we have guest houses with tea-making facilities, the taking of holidays at exotic locations any time of the year; and buildings on Blackhorse Street swept away in the 1985/6 rebuilding of the bus station.

Wartime

Both Pictures: There are one or two cheerful faces amongst this group of children at Turton Station (left), but on the whole their faces sum up the bewilderment and anxiety they must have felt. The date was September 1st 1939 and war with Germany was very imminent. The government expected huge casualties from bombing, a quarter of a million in the first week alone. Therefore children were being evacuated from major cities. This group of evacuees had arrived from Manchester to be billeted with local people of Turton. The greatest fear of all was gas attack and gas mask boxes are visible here and there, along with identity labels. Younger children may have regarded it all as a bit of an adventure, but for the older ones the routines of gas mask practice and air-raid shelter drill must have held out the prospect of a terrifying future. As the 'Bolton Evening News' put it, with its ironic caption over a picture of tiny tots being evacuated, 'Civilisation -1939'.

A happier scene is depicted on the photograph below, of October 1939, which seems to show that the evacuees have settled in and begun to enjoy themselves. The see-saw at Egerton playing fields is proving popular and it looks as if a game of football is about to get underway. No doubt everyone wanted the lads with the steel-toed clogs on their side! It is likely that most of these children soon returned to Manchester, for the heavy bombing did not at first materialise. Between September 1939 and April 1940, a period known as the 'phoney war', there were no air-raids to speak of and most children returned to their families. The 'Blitz', however, began in earnest in September 1940, causing another wave of evacuation. Bolton, in fact, turned out to be a relatively safe place for evacuees. Five tons of bombs fell on Bolton, causing 17 deaths and 113 injuries. By far the greatest number of these came in one incident. On October 12th 1941, two 500 kilo bombs fell on Punch Street and Ardwick Street, with 11 deaths and 64 people injured. This was a tragedy for all concerned, but an earlier incident, in January 1941, could have resulted in a major disaster. Bombs dropped just to the east and the west of the Odeon, pitting the walls with fragments. A packed house of 1800 people blithely sat through all this, watching Bob Hope in 'Ghost Breaker' to the end.

Bolton Evening News

Both pictures: This is a happy occasion for these smiling and charming young ladies in a photograph that seems to date from the late 1950s. The occasion is not known, but the distinguished looking gentleman in the middle is perhaps handing out awards to these ambulance workers of the Bolton Division. What is known is that they were members of Civil Defence, of which the ambulance service was just one branch. Civil Defence grew out of the bombing of towns and cities during World War Two. The ordinary public services could not alone deal with the deaths, injuries and devastation in heavily bombed areas. Therefore men and women were urged to become part-time firefighters or ambulance drivers, or undertake a host of other worthwhile tasks. By 1942, in Bolton, there were around 8000 volunteer Civil Defence workers. By far the biggest branch was Air-Raid Precaution (ARP) which contained around 7000 of these. Each street or zone had its Air-Raid Warden to enforce blackout regulations or to assist in getting people to the shelters if the sirens sounded. Other Civil Defence workers joined the casualty and rescue branch of ARP. After the war, the government was anxious to continue with Civil Defence. The war had scarcely ended before Winston Churchill was speaking of the 'Iron Curtain' dividing Europe. The Cold War between the USA and the USSR had begun. The shadow of nuclear war fell across the world and in Britain it was felt that the expertise and organisation of Civil Defence was worth preserving. In Bolton, a big exhibition was staged at the Walker Memorial Institute in November 1951, opened by the Mayor, Alderman Dunning. An illuminated bus toured Bolton. The aim was to gather 1500 recruits and the Mayor himself enrolled as No 510. Although the underlying purpose was a serious one, the social side of Civil Defence was also stressed, with quizzes, competitions, dances etc. The photograph shows a children's Christmas party about to commence, a very smart and dressed up affair, with the Queen's portrait prominent. The 1960s brought controversy. Some argued that Civil Defence could do nothing in the face of the devastation of a nuclear attack and that people were merely being lulled into a false sense of security. Fortunately this was never put to the test and the Cold War ended in the late 1980s.

Nevertheless, we still live in an uncertain world in 1998.

Below: 'Give him one in the mouth' was precisely what Bolton people would have liked to have done to Hitler, Mussolini and Hirohito in person. Therefore it was a clever idea to channel people's anger into throwing money in the mouths of their effigies in aid of the Mayor of Bolton's fund for prisoners-of-war. These novel collecting 'boxes' were designed by Fred Windsor (standing to the left of the photograph) at the First Aid Central Depot in Blackhorse Street and shortly afterwards they were set up in prominent positions in Bolton. The date was May 1942 and the images were powerful and arresting. This was a pre-television age and the government and other agencies had to rely upon getting their message across through posters on the streets or on public transport. Readers who lived through that difficult period will remember such government messages as 'Dig For Victory', or 'Careless Talk Costs Lives'. No doubt Bolton folk responded generously to this appeal and the allusion to Hong Kong, where 12,000 prisoners had fallen into Japanese hands at Christmas 1941. Sadly, for reasons best known to themselves, the Japanese prevented thousands of Red Cross parcels, from reaching their unfortunate prisoners.

Right: All manner of initiatives were launched to get the public involved in the war effort. In so doing, it was hoped that the publicity would generate more cash to help meet the colossal expense of fighting the Second World War. The photograph shows an RAF 'open day' in June 1944 and an aircraft man pointing out the controls of a typical bomber. It has to be said that the visitors look a bit bemused and their eyes seem to be firmly focused on the terrifying looking bomb nose up to the left. Nevertheless such schemes did pay off and astonishing amounts were raised by towns and cities who 'adopted' battleships or air squadrons, as well as loyally supporting their local regiments. In May 1943, for example, the 'Wings for Victory' appeal week was launched in Bolton.

A Hudson aircraft was erected outside the Town Hall and there was a colourful full-scale parade and march past. Bolton's ambitious money-raising scheme in 1944, £11/2 million, is clearly stated on one of the posters in the picture, along with an appeal to local pride - 'Don't let us down'. The 'Salute the Soldier' poster was more of a nationally based appeal for people to buy such things as war bonds.

Bolton Evening News

Bolton Evening News

Both pages: Happy faces, waving flags and decorations. This was the celebratory scene in the winding room of No 8 mill, Musgrave Spinning Co, Bute Street, on May 7th 1945. 'It's all over', was the message. Well, not quite. The war in Europe did not officially end until May 8th 1945, 'VE Day', but these Bolton workers clearly knew what was afoot and the celebrations had begun. However, it is easy to get a misleading picture of 'VE Day' as one of unrestrained joy. People were glad enough that the Second World War was over in Europe, but this feeling was mingled with uncertainty in many Bolton households. Japan was fighting on and some women had received no news of their menfolk literally for years. Sadness, of course, might have been the prevalent feeling in the Bolton households where it was known that the menfolk were not returning at all.

The official announcement was made over the wireless by Prime Minister Churchill at 3pm. Victory peals rang out from St Peter's Church and people gathered outside the Town Hall in the expectation of some public address from the steps, but none was forthcoming. Hasty and impromptu street parties were set in motion and the photograph shows the residents of Bashall Street 'letting their hair down'. Great effort has gone into decorating the street and both young and old appear to be enjoying themselves. Understandably, there is a shortage of young men for the dancing. Elsewhere, celebrations took on a different slant. At Farnworth Mill, for example, an effigy of Hitler, complete with

Bolton Evening News

Bolton Evening News

baskets and bits of timber. A few fireworks went off at night and then 'VE Day' was all over.

Two days later, however, a large crowd assembled outside the Town Hall for Bolton's united service of thanksgiving. The photograph of this event conveys the impression of a solemn occasion, with the mayor and other dignitaries on the steps and a relay system conveying the service to the crowd. The proximity of the War Memorial, to the left of Victoria Square, must have added poignancy to it all. The Second World War cost the lives of around 1500 people from Bolton and district, many of them being soldiers belonging to the Royal North Lancs Regiment. The period around 'VE Day' really was a time of thanksgiving for some, but for others it marked the moment when their worst fears were realised. Doris Rostron, for example, had heard nothing of her husband since his ship had been torpedoed off Gibraltar in 1942. It was around 'VE Day' that she received a telegram saying that he had just been demobilised. On the other hand, the parents of Staff Sergeant John Ellison, of Horwich, were receiving the news that their son had been killed in March, during airborne landings near the Rhine.

paint can, was strung outside on a crane. In the evening, there were hastily arranged victory dances at the Spinner's Hall and the Astoria. If it was all a little low-key, this was partly to do with another problem. What were people to celebrate with? The announcement of the end of the war in Europe did not miraculously end shortages and rationing. Bolton housewives made their daily raid on the shops to find the usual situation- little food and no tobacco at all. An attempt to build a victory beacon at Old Links Golf Course was hampered by the fact that the only fuel available was a few old broken

Bolton School - the route to excellence

To the people of Bolton, the badges of the pupils who attend Bolton School will be a familiar sight. Both the girls' and the boys' badges include: the rose, for Lancashire; the open book, to represent learning; and a wreath of roses, to signify honour. The boys' coat of arms also bears the inscription "Mutare Vel Timere Sperno", which means "I spurn to change or to fear". This is a highly appropriate motto, as the basic principles upon which education in Bolton was founded have remained unchanged through the centuries, with a commitment to making the very highest standard of education accessible to all.

Inevitably, there have been changes in school organisation, and the most significant and far-reaching change of all must be the amalgamation, in 1913, of the High School for Girls with the Bolton Grammar School for Boys. Of the two schools, the Grammar School for Boys was by far the older, having existed since 1516.

The High School for Girls had come into existence comparatively recently, on October 1st, 1877. To fund the girls' school, its founders each guaranteed a sum of £200; 'an efficient lady teacher', Miss Eliza Kean, was appointed, at a salary of £100 a year, to teach Reading, Writing, Arithmetic, Grammar, Geography, English, History, Needlework, French

and Latin; the schoolroom was in the Mechanics' Institute, and the 1877 intake consisted of twenty-two girls. The fee was four guineas a year and the school was open to all girls, regardless of class. It was one of the very earliest public day-schools for girls; the first had been opened in North London in 1850, and many towns found the concept of providing education for girls difficult to accept. Bolton had

Top: Boys at the entrance to School from main quadrangle, 1946. *Left:* The Headmasters' Lawn, the Old Swimming Baths and Groundsman's House in 1955.

between the two schools led to a healthy rivalry. The girls' school lost no time in attaining academic excellence, under the guidance of a series of distinguished Headmistresses. In 1880 Miss Kean was succeeded by Mrs Sarah Corbett, who had her own school in Silverwell House; these two schools amalgamated and moved to 39 Chorley New Road. Mrs Corbett, nee Woodhead, had been one of the first three students at Girton College, Cambridge; her successor, Miss Vokins, was one of the first students of Newnham, and Miss Johnson, who was Headmistress from 1887 to 1893, also graduated from Newnham. Bolton girls began winning places at Cambridge in 1890, and have continued the tradition ever since.

no such prejudices, and the school soon established an excellent reputation. At the Girls' first Prizegiving in January 1879 it was commented by Mr W Hart that "there was a great want in this town of a school similar to the Bolton Boys' Grammar School for the advantage of the girls." The excellent example set by the boys educated there may well have helped in predisposing the people of Bolton to welcome education for girls as well, and certainly the inevitable comparisons

Bolton Grammar School for Boys is believed to be one of the oldest schools in Lancashire. Although

Top left: *Visit of Russian Educationalists, May 1957; from left, Miss M. Higginson (Headmistress), Mr B. Harrison, Madame Tovetkova, Mr Dadashev, and Mr F.R. Poskitt (Headmaster).* **Below:** *Girls working in one of the science laboratories in 1957.*

bureaucratic changes and the changing beliefs and traditions over the centuries led to fluctuations in the school's financial circumstances and academic standing at various times, overall it managed to flourish, moving from its original Tudor building with white-washed wall and a thatched roof to new premises during the seventeenth century, and moving again in 1899, shortly after its amalgamation with Bolton High School for Boys, into the premises at Westbourne which it occupied until 1932. This third move was made possible by William Hesketh Lever. The School's association with the Lever name can be traced back to before the school's first relocation in the seventeenth century, when Robert Lever seems to have become involved with the maintenance of the school at its old site as well as making preparations for its re-founding at the new site. Under the foundation deeds, Robert Lever was to be regarded as the founder and his kin were to be preferred as governors. William Hesketh Lever's precise kinship to Robert Lever, if any, is obscure; however, as a Non-Conformist he strongly approved of the amalgamation between Bolton Boys' Grammar School and Bolton High School for Boys, which had been founded by his own master, W T Mason, also a Non-Conformist. William Lever agreed to help the school by putting up £5,000 and

Above: Quiet study in the School in 1950. Left: The Old Boys Association - Diamond Jubilee Dinner December 17th 1955.

being co-opted as governor, and his deep commitment to the school was demonstrated by his regular attendance at governors' meetings. In 1899 he bought the freehold of Westbourne and offered it to the governors of the school, and he also financed the necessary building alterations. Shortly after the school opened at Westbourne, there were 102 boys on the register, and by 1902 there were 166. The increase in numbers then halted when fees were raised to ten guineas for senior boys and eight guineas for juniors. It was the policy of the school to keep fee increases to a minimum, to keep the school within the means of the lower middle classes. William Lever's financial assistance to the school continued in many guises, including the provision of a swimming pool, and the funding of scholarships.

William Lever appears to have had in mind a plan to amalgamate the girls' and boys' schools in 1910, and by 1913 his plans were becoming more detailed. He envisaged completely rebuilding the

Above: A geography class with M.W. Bagot, 1952.
Below: The Woodwork room pictured in 1946.

Bolton Grammar School, with one wing for boys and one for girls; boys and girls were to be taught separately, although for some lessons, such as swimming and gymnastics, the same teachers might be timetabled to teach both the boys' classes and the girls' classes. Other buildings were also planned, including a U-shaped building which was to extend to Chorley New Road. Plans were drawn up, and a new name was sought for the joint establishment; a suggestion that it should be called University College was rejected as it was felt this would be misleading, and finally the name Bolton School was agreed upon, with the terms Boys' Division and Girls' Division to be used when it was necessary to distinguish between the two. Unfortunately the rebuilding work was delayed by the outbreak of war, but the re-founding of the School went ahead and Bolton School came into existence on 1 April 1915.

The headmaster of the Boys' Division at the time of the re-endowment was W G Lipscomb, who was Head from 1903 and until his retirement in 1924. Whilst the headmistress of the Girls' Division was Miss Olivia Dymond. Miss

Dymond, another Newnham graduate, was the longest serving Head in the history of the School, holding the post from 1893 to 1919, during which time she achieved excellent results throughout. Her attention to detail is legendary, as is her devotion to duty; when a week's holiday was proclaimed in honour of the Coronation in 1911, she felt so strongly that her examination candidates could not afford to take time off from their studies that she gave up her own holiday to stay with them! It was she, too, who introduced school uniform and compulsory games. Meanwhile, one result of the war was a lack of male teachers, and the Boys' Division began to employ schoolmistresses, who were addressed by the boys as 'Madam' but were nonetheless referred to as 'masters'.

Construction of the new buildings finally began in 1924 and continued throughout the period between the wars. By the time the Second World War broke out, Bolton School was well

Above: Clermont-Ferraud Exchange children, August 1954 - photographed at Hall I'Th' Wood.

established, and boys and girls share a common store of wartime memories. The school buildings were used for fire-watching, with two members of staff on duty in each Division every evening from dusk onwards. Those on fire watch were treated to bread, butter and cheese for supper, and in the morning the fire-watchers from the Girls' Division would join the fire-watchers from the Boys' Division for breakfast. Lord Haslam (Chairman of the Joint Governing Body from July 1990 until June 1997) has recalled that, as a pupil on fire watch in the Boys' Division, he used to be kept supplied with cakes baked by the girls in their cookery lessons. There were also opportunities for the boys and girls to become actively involved in wartime activities; for instance, when it was announced that evacuees from the Channel Islands were to arrive in Bolton, the Scouts were aided by a group of girls who spent two days repairing and furnishing two large empty houses, and making them ready for occupation by the evacuees.

It was not until well after the end of the Second World War, in 1965, that the main wings of the School were completed, fulfilling William Hesketh Lever's stated aim of having 'the Grammar School housed in a properly designed and planned building, built expressly for the purpose'. Since then, more building works have been planned and carried out. In the 1950s a new sports level was created, and the Tillotson Pavilion was erected through the generosity of the Tillotson family, although unfortunately a more ambitious scheme to merge three levels to create a huge playing field had to be curtailed because of lack of funds. Funding for projects has come from various sources: a grant from the Industrial Society financed the construction of a new Chemistry Block for the Boys' Division, adjacent to the main school buildings, and this was opened in 1958. In the early 1970s the Trustees of Bridge Street Methodist Chapel presented to the School an organ which was made for the Chapel in 1885, and costs of installing the organ in the Great Hall in the Girls' Division were met by the New Lever Trustees. In 1982 the Leverhulme Pavilion at Oldfield was opened by Lord Leverhulme; in addition to games changing areas, this building houses a fully equipped kitchen provided through the generosity of Mrs Vause, Chairman of the Bolton School Trustees, and the Girl's Division Parents' Association. Lord

Below: Girls and staff admiring their handicrafts during the 80th Birthday celebrations, 1957.

Leverhulme was also responsible for the acquisition of the equestrian centre on Ladybridge Lane which has been converted into the Scout Group's new headquarters, Brookside. Major additions to the School's facilities in recent years include the ultra-modern, purpose-built Arts & Conference Centre which offers tremendous scope for music, arts and drama productions, and Patterdale Hall, an outdoor pursuits centre situated at the heart of a 300 acre estate at the southern end of Ullswater, in the Lake District. Throughout the centuries, it was the tradition of both the boys' and the girls' schools to offer a good education to all children, irrespective of the family's financial circumstances, and this has not changed. Currently, one third of the School's pupils receive assistance with fees. Pupils, who number over 2,000, are drawn from a wide area encompassing urban and rural Lancashire, Cheshire and Greater Manchester; a network of School coach services covers twenty-one routes over a twenty-five mile radius of the School. The School caters for boys and girls from the age of four; entrance to the Senior Schools is at the age of eleven, and to the Sixth Forms at the age of sixteen. The results of pupils at GCSE and A Level consistently place Bolton School amongst the top independent schools in the country, with a high percentage of Sixth Form students going on to University; both the Boys' and the Girls' Division are strongly represented at Oxford and Cambridge. The academic excellence of the School is established beyond a doubt, as is its

Top left: Visit of Field Marshall Viscount Montgomery, January 1954. Standing from left: Mr F.R. Poskitt (Headmaster), Viscount Montgomery, Mr R. Booth and Lord Leverhulme. *Below:* Pupils from the Girls' School working in the library in 1957.

outstanding pastoral care, which focuses on developing the talents and character of each individual within a framework of good discipline, and fostering an environment where pupils treat each other with respect, courtesy and consideration and learn to assume responsibility and leadership so that they are ready to take their places responsibly in society. It is important to the School that students enjoy their school learning experience, and they are encouraged to make full use of the superb facilities for outdoor pursuits, sport, music and drama which the School has to offer. Boys and girls are taught separately, but extra curricular activities, particularly in music and drama, involve both Boys' and Girls' Divisions. A highly-acclaimed orchestra composed of musically-gifted pupils from both Divisions gives regular concerts during the Autumn and Spring terms, and the Choir, the Chamber Choir and the Wind Band are all joint ventures.

Bolton School has also explored ways to extend the use of its excellent facilities so that the community at large can benefit from them. The Arts and Conference Centre, whilst remaining primarily a School facility, is used for business and social activities during evenings, weekends and school holidays. With two magnificent Great Halls and a purpose-built theatre which are available for hire, it has become one of Bolton's most popular venues for exhibitions, musical and social functions and even weddings.

Similarly, Patterdale Hall, the School's outdoor pursuits centre, operates as a commercial residential centre when not in use for groups from the School, lending itself to a variety of uses, from providing a base for fieldwork studies

to a leading a week's structured team-building programme.

These ventures are run by Bolton School Services Limited, whose initiatives also include the extension of the School coach services into a commercial coach service, available for hire for outings and holidays, and the organising of Bolton School Summer Schools over the summer. In recent years these have included outdoor pursuits, ceramics and creative crafts. Schemes such as this mean that the maximum benefit is derived from the excellent facilities which the School has at its disposal, as well as generating extra income. The primary function of Bolton School Services Limited is to ensure that the School's charitable status is preserved, and any profits raised can be channelled back into the financial upkeep of the school and its facilities. As an independent school, Bolton School is reliant on fee income, and is also committed to providing Foundation Grants and bursaries to those pupils who would not otherwise be able to attend the School. This is a commitment to which it has adhered throughout its long history.

*Above: Lord James of Rusholme and Len Vickers (School Captain) at Boys' Division Speech Day in 1960. **Left:** Boys' Division Speech Day, July 1960 - Televised in the Gym.*

Sporting life

This 'bird's eye view', from around 1966 captures an arena with a host of memories for many Boltonians. Burnden Park was not the first home for Bolton Wanderers, who began their life playing at Pikes Lane from 1881. This proved to be too small and in 1893 an offer was made to the Gas Committee to lease a five acre site. This became Burnden Park and in 1894 shares were issued in the Bolton Wanderers Football and Athletic Co Ltd. The opening event was a big athletics meeting in August 1895, accompanied by entertainments such as performing dogs, stilt walking and trapeze diving - all to the accompaniment of the Halliwell Brass Band. Football, however, was to be the staple diet of Burnden Park. From the first Football League match there, against Everton in September 1895, some stirring and memorable encounters took place and supporters of the 'Trotters' will all have their memories of joy and despair. Not many will be left now of the largest attendance ever at Burnden, a staggering 69,912 in 1933, although more will remember the ill-fated game of 1946 when barriers collapsed and 33 died. The Wanderers moved to the new Reebok Stadium in 1997, but memories of Burnden Park live on.

Both pictures: The reputation of Bolton Wanderers as cup-fighters used to be second to none. Even though visits to Wembley in cup competitions have become comparatively rare of late, the Wanderers have contested seven FA Cup Finals, a record that many other clubs can only envy. Victories came in 1923, 1926, 1929 and 1958; defeats in 1894, 1904 and 1953. Not all these were played at Wembley, of course and the club featured in the first ever Wembley final, that of 1923. This may still rank as the most famous final of all. The pitch was swamped by a crowd of 200,000 which had somehow struggled in. Seemingly, order was restored by some kind of superman, the famous 'policeman on the white horse'. The Wanderers eventually went on to beat West Ham (2-0) and in those heady days of the 1920s, Bolton lifted the FA Cup again in 1926 and 1929. Anyone taking a casual glance at the photograph might think that this was one of the club's triumphant returns as FA Cup holders. In fact, it is quite another cup being paraded through the crowded streets of Bolton in 1945. Team Captain Harry Hubbick, surrounded by team mates, is proudly displaying the Football League War Cup from the open roof of the motor coach. The Wanderers had won the Northern section of this competition by beating Manchester United over two legs, the final one at Old Trafford being watched by a huge crowd of 57,395. Then Bolton had gone on to win the national trophy by beating Chelsea (2-1) at Chelsea.

This must have given a war-weary Bolton a much needed lift and the crowded streets give evidence to this. This long line of people outside Burnden Park shows that 'cup fever' was alive and well in Bolton in 1954. The picture provides a social commentary on the standard dress of the time and the 'vintage' buggy in the background looks far from comfortable.

These supporters were queuing to get their hands on some of the 3000 ground tickets which had been returned unsold from Sheffield Wednesday for a Sixth Round Cup replay. Alas, this game was lost and so there was to be no return to Wembley one year after the epic battle with Blackpool in 1953. Nevertheless, 1958 saw the Wanderers lift the Cup again, at the expense of Manchester United, providing a last appearance in the Wembley arena for that Bolton 'legend', Nat Lofthouse.

Bird's eye view

This aerial survey over Bolton, probably from 1949, seems to have been done from a higher elevation than many later aerial views. As a result, much more has been encompassed than usual, although detail is less clear. The overall impression is one of industrialisation, with a good many terrace rows and a fair sprinkling of factory chimneys. Almost in the bottom right-hand corner, Trinity Street station can be located. The railway line sweeps up the right hand side of the photograph, past a gasholder, towards Bury. A very distinctive feature at the top, towards the right, is the 'Back o' th' Bank' Power Station. The straightest road on view, disappearing towards the top, is Blackburn Road. The Town Hall is visible in the bottom left-hand quarter, with the arc of Le Mans Crescent to the rear. Behind that again is Moor Lane bus station. Just below this point, towards the bottom, is the chimney of the Royal George mill. Sainsburys now stands on this site. A close examination of the photograph will reveal plenty of other changes for those with keen eyes and good memories.

Left: The dominating features of this aerial view of Bolton are Queen's Park and the Town Hall. The former top right, was opened in 1866 as a 'playground' for Boltonians at a time when green spaces were vital in the midst of industrial settings. The Town Hall is prominent to the left/centre of the picture. The block of buildings facing the front of the Town Hall, at the left edge of the picture, are in their 'undeveloped' state. This block was opened as the Arndale Centre in 1971 and so the view pre-dates this by a few years. No Boltonian should take the Town Hall for granted, for visitors are invariably impressed at its style and grandeur. The Town Hall was built at a cost of around £170,000 and was opened in 1873. It was designed in Classical style by William Hill of Leeds and George Woodhouse of Bolton. The graceful arc of the much admired Le Mans Crescent can be seen behind the Town Hall. The Crescent contains many important public departments and was officially opened in 1939. Its creation formed part of a major scheme which included an extended Town Hall, incorporating a new Civic Centre. The cost this time was nearer £1 million.

Below: The gasholders at the top of the photograph, alongside Queen's Park, are a useful starting point for an examination of this aerial view, taken in 1966. Moving downwards one can find Moor Lane Bus Station nestling behind the distinctive curve of the Le Mans Crescent.

In front of this is the impressive edifice of the Town Hall and the roads flanking this part of the picture, moving from top to bottom, are Great Moor Street on the left and Deansgate on the right. Deansgate can be followed downwards into historic Churchgate, with the Parish Church of St Peter's at the very bottom of the photograph, on the right. St Peter's was consecrated in 1871, after being rebuilt at a cost of £45,000.

The old church, built in the early 15th Century, was completely demolished in this process, although the floor still remains under the present building. The grounds of the Parish Church extend leftwards as far as the Church Institute. Moving upwards from this point and also bearing left one finds the Silverwell Street Drill Hall, which was demolished as recently as 1997.

Great Moor Street, almost as if drawn by a ruler, bisects the bottom part of this aerial view of 1964. Both the name of this street and that of Moor Lane, are reminders of the time when moorlands once flourished across these particular areas. Perhaps equally strange is to consider the Town Hall area (in the centre towards the top) as it was in the early nineteenth century - a pleasant meadow containing a stream and an orchard. However, some of the most striking features on the picture illustrate the industrial growth since those rural days. Almost in the centre, alongside Great Moor Street, stands the Pin Mill complex, comprising the Royal George and Sovereign Mills. The Mather Street Mill can be seen at the bottom, towards the right. The railway line in the bottom right-hand corner belonged to the Bolton and Leigh Railway Company. This opened in 1828, making it one of the earliest lines in the country. By 1831 it was carrying both passengers and goods to Liverpool. The line curves its way up to the left towards Great Moor Street. Here, near Pin Mill, was the terminus. Both the line and this station were closed to passengers in 1954.

THE CLEAN AIR ACT OF THE 1960s RESTORED MANY OF BOLTONS' FINEST BUILDINGS TO THEIR NATURAL COLOURS

Individual buildings are often the key to dating an aerial picture and the presence of two important landmarks indicates that this photograph was taken before 1969. On the far right, just below centre, stands the Church Institute, demolished in 1969. The Bolton brewers of Magee Marshall had their bonded warehouse in the corner of the large space which accommodated the Wholesale Fruit and Vegetable Market. This can be located at a little distance below the Town Hall and again this bonded warehouse was demolished in 1969.

Just above it is the site on which was built the present day Octagon Theatre. Other notable buildings are the Commercial Hotel, to the right of the Town Hall and the Lido Cinema on Bradshawgate. Both these are of a distinctive white colour. Buildings like this must have really stood out once against surroundings that had been blackened by generations of smoke and soot from factory and house chimneys. The Clean Air Acts of the 1960s, linked with the sand blasting process to clean stonework, restored many of Bolton's public buildings to their natural colour. This surprised some people who had assumed that black was the natural colour of stone, as even moorland outcrops were blackened from industrial 'fall-out'.

Events & occasions

Bolton Evening News

Above: World War Two was not quite yet over, so little warning was given of the visit of King George VI and Queen Elizabeth to Bolton, on March 8th 1945. Nevertheless, news had got round and the pavements were thronged with cheering crowds along the royal route into Bolton. Schoolchildren had been given a holiday and around 7000 of them formed part of the huge crowd in Victoria Square. At the Town Hall, the royal couple were greeted by the Mayor and Mayoress, Alderman and Mrs Bradley. They then had lunch with a distinguished group of civilian and military figures, but following the usual war-time custom, the meal was an austerity one provided by the staff of the British Restaurant. Just prior to departure, the King and Queen insisted on breaking their tight schedule by taking time to chat to a group of wounded soldiers, accompanied by nurses, from Townleys Hospital. The photograph shows this about to take place. Amongst the soldiers spoken to were RSM Garside of Danesbury Road, wounded at the Falaise Gap and Guardsman Hession of Bangor Street,

wounded in Holland. Their majesties received a rousing send off on a day which brought a spot of colour into those grim wartime years.

Facing page both pictures: The big moment is imminent as the royal cavalcade of cars approaches the Town Hall on May 20th 1938. This photograph captures the massive enthusiasm and excitement engendered by this visit to Bolton of King George VI and Queen Elizabeth on the fourth day of their Lancashire tour. Thousands of people are packed into Victoria Square and some of them have found vantage points that would give modern security men nightmares. At least six have found their way on to the roof of the Town Hall itself, whilst another group clings precariously to a roof top opposite. In the blue and gold enclosure in front of the Town Hall steps, the official reception party awaits, including Lord Derby and the Mayor and Mayoress, Alderman and Mrs Halstead. Opposite are the extremely smart ranks of Duke of Lancaster's Own Yeomanry.

Bolton Evening News

Bolton Evening News

This particular visit took place in warm sunshine and the huge interest it aroused was reflected in the clamorous crowds which lined the royal route. It was estimated, for example, that 6000 people lined Moor Lane, cheering and waving flags. The Queen responded with smiles and her characteristic wave, whilst the King bowed gravely. The visit was a fleeting one, for after arriving at the Town Hall at about 12.30pm, the royal couple departed at shortly before 1pm. Nevertheless, the King had time to

express his admiration of the Civic Centre and enquire about the state of trade. The Queen, chatting to the Mayoress, commented on Bolton's wonderful reception. Those present were later to praise Queen Elizabeth's 'spontaneous friendliness' and King George VI's 'simple dignity'.

An unrehearsed departure from the tight schedule caused much interest at the time. Before entering the Town Hall, the royal couple had made their way across to chat to a group of World War One veterans, some of them badly disabled. The photograph shows the King admiring one of the many medals on display. One of the veterans, James Grant, had served as a Warrant Engineer on 'HMS Cumberland', having been a shipmate to the King himself. To Mr Grant's surprise, the King recognised him. The Queen was concerned about how long the veterans might have been waiting and was pleased to see that chairs had been provided. A special wave was reserved for the veterans as the royal car later departed along Newport Street. The crowds which lined the outward journey, through Farnworth towards Ringley, gave the royal party a rapturous send-off.

Bolton Evening News

Both pictures: 'E II R' - these 12 foot high letters, erected on the lawn at the corner of Victoria Square and Old Hall Street South, seemed to sum it all up. It was May 1953 and preparations were in hand everywhere to mark the approaching Coronation of Queen Elizabeth II in an unforgettable way. This event really was a landmark. The new Elizabethan Age was dawning and it was time to shake off the drab years of post-war-austerity. The crowning of a young queen captured everyone's imagination and the atmosphere was full of new-found optimism. Those who were young at that time may well remember the launching of a new magazine, 'The Young Elizabethan', which seemed to capture the spirit of it all. The massive royal emblem on the photograph is being examined with a mixture of admiration and caution by these passers-by. Perhaps this was part of an outing for these youngsters to look at the Bolton decorations, for as the great day approached, public buildings in the town centre increasingly offered a colourful display of bunting, flags and streamers.

Nor was there any shortage of patriotism amongst the ordinary citizens of Bolton. These smiling ladies, who were employed in one of the cardrooms at Cannon Bros, had made a real effort to enter into the spirit of things by festooning the ceiling of their mill with balloons, paper chains and flags.
Continued overleaf

From previous page
As they were doing it they may have been humming along to the big 'hit' melody of the time, 'Elizabethan Serenade'. Many may remember that evocative piece of music, which seemed to be on the radio every two minutes. Wherever the people of Bolton came together to work - shops, mills, schools, hospitals - imaginative minds and busy hands produced decorations that were fit for a new monarch and a new era. Community spirit is always seen at its best on such occasions and the residents of many Bolton streets got together in 1953 to see what they could do. Here the residents of Reservoir Street are seen at work on May 29th 1953. Young and old are taking advantage of the sunshine to get the flags and bunting in position and no doubt a street party was planned for Coronation Day itself. Reservoir Street was full of patriotic emblems and it is easy to forget just how loyal the country was to the institution of monarchy in 1953. There was no hint of modern day cynicism in ordinary people's attitudes towards the Crown. This was a time when the National Anthem was played and sung to, at the end of all public performances. People usually stood, sometimes to attention. Anyone who made a dash for the door was frowned upon, even if he or she had a bus to catch!

Bolton Evening News

Judging by the way everyone is well wrapped up, those jugs of hot tea are very welcome. Nevertheless it is smiles all round at Barrow Bridge, which was at its height as a beauty spot when the picture was taken in the 1930s. Dean Mills had once stood at Barrow Bridge and their owners, Robert Gardner and Thomas Bazley, had interesting ideas. At a time when most cotton workers endured pitiful conditions in mills, with long hours and low wages, Gardner and Bazley believed in having a happy workforce. Hence, in 1835, they created a model industrial village. The mills contained hot baths and dining rooms equipped with newspapers. Good quality housing was built and a Co-operative Shop, which sold goods cheaply. An institute was built in 1846 for educational, recreational and religious activities. The experiment was over by the end of the century and Dean Mills were demolished in 1913. After that, Barrow Bridge became a playground for Boltonians, with a boating lake, fairground and tea room. You could even buy Barrow Bridge rock! Times have moved on since this happy photograph was taken. The lake has been filled in to provide a car park for visitors to what is now a conservation area.

Both pictures: June 2nd 1953 was a much awaited date on the calendar, for it marked the Coronation of Queen Elizabeth II. The sense of a new era beginning, along with a chance for people to 'let their hair down', coloured the countrywide celebrations and Bolton fully entered into the spirit of it all. Naturally the British weather rose to the occasion. June 2nd 1953 was dull and cold, with squally bursts of rain, but people were determined to enjoy themselves. The Coronation ceremony in London took place in the morning and was televised. However, most homes did not have a television in 1953 and so it was a matter of people gathering wherever one was available. Claremont Baptist Church set up a television for communal viewing and around 140 watched. Over 100 attended St Augustine's School at Tonge Moor (left) for the same purpose. The screens were small; the images were black-and-white and of poor quality; but anyone who watched that day will not have forgotten the experience of having been part of a significant national event.

Then, for the rest of the day, the people of Bolton cut loose in all manner of celebrations. Scores of street parties reflected community spirit as well as patriotism, although the miserable weather forced some to adapt to indoor versions. Bull Lane won the £20 first prize for best decorated street, with Manley Terrace in Astley Bridge second and Nevis Grove third. The photograph of the happy residents of Bull Lane (above) gives some idea of the sheer volume of the decorations. Passers-by must have been hit by a 'wall' of colour, as even the curtains of the houses were red, white and blue. The Meredith Street Coronation Queen, Norma Gates, has pride of place in the second photograph (overleaf, bottom). Among her attendants are her two brothers, Ronald and Barrie, dressed in guards' uniforms and wearing busbies created from their mother's old black coat. Norma has a full retinue of charming young ladies to accompany her and no doubt their 'natty' headgear is in the appropriate patriotic colours. Elsewhere, Little Bo Peep and perhaps Prince Charming are putting in an appearance in a photograph that has captured a treasured memory for anyone who was one of these Meredith Street youngsters in 1953.

The children's party organised by the women's section of Darcy Lever Conservative Club took place on the weekend before Coronation Day, but the celebratory mood is very evident in this picture. There is an interesting range of hats and it looks as if the ladies on the right are about to do the honours in serving up the party 'goodies'. One can imagine the state of those tablecloths after the consumption of all the pop and buns, not to mention the mountains of washing up. Every child received a Coronation cup in 1953, mainly through the local education authorities. These were very tastefully embellished and a good many Coronation cups are on view in this photograph.

Continued overleaf

Bolton Evening News

From previous page
How many of these still survive today? The casual manner in which the two children at the front are holding their cups seems to suggest a short life-span for these particular souvenirs.

The residents of De Lacy Drive (above) braved the elements to get outside for this photograph. The general wetness of the road and pavements gives a good indication of the miserable weather that day. The number of overcoats show that it was not exactly 'flaming June'. Nevertheless, spirits were not dampened and the people of Bolton fully intended to make this a memorable day. This cheerful bunch are giving what appears to be the De Lacy Drive 'war whoop', although the dog seems unimpressed. On a fashion footnote, short trousers are much in evidence. This was a time when boys wore short trousers until they were about 13 years old. How would the trend-setting young teenagers of today have coped with that?

The fashion market for children still lay in the future in 1953. Street parties were a form of 'do-it-yourself' entertainment which worked wonders for community spirit. However, there were also plenty of events laid on for people on June 2nd 1953. At the Grand Theatre (right) a group of local children, 'The Dinky Dots', put on a Coronation Spectacular' entitled 'To See The Queen'. There was a spectacle of an unintentional nature when the decorations along Bradshawgate, close to the old Queen's Cinema, went up in flames after coming into contact with a cracked neon sign. At the Albert Hall, the big Coronation Dance had been a sell-out well in advance of the day. The evening fireworks display at Queen's Park attracted an estimated 15,000 people. The activity was not all confined to the central area of Bolton. At Farnworth, for example, there was a torch-light procession, headed by the Eagley Mills Band. All-in-all, Coronation Day provided an unforgettable experience for the citizens of Bolton.

If it was cold and showery for the Coronation celebrations of June 1953, it was positively pouring down for the next royal occasion in Bolton. This was the visit of Queen Elizabeth II and the Duke of Edinburgh on October 22nd 1954, the second day of their Lancashire tour. The clock at Trinity Street station shows 10am precisely on the photograph overleaf, which also shows the red carpet, the shrubs and the heavily decorated platform three. The Mayor, Alderman Flanagan (partially concealed by the Queen) is about to present her to local dignitaries and Prince Philip can be seen to the rear.

From the railway station, the royal cavalcade of cars passed along Trinity Street, Bradshawgate, Great Moor

Street and Newport Street. Crowds had been gathering since early morning, undeterred by the heavy rain. The sound of their cheers mingled with the bells of Bolton Parish Church. Girl Guides of the Bolton Division lined Trinity Street and a party of three to four year olds from Holy Trinity School took up the coveted places beneath the wall of Trinity Church. A special effort was made to get children to the front and this photograph shows their cheerful faces in spite of the weather that day. Although the rain had stopped briefly on the arrival of the royal party at the station, the number of raincoats, hats and wellingtons on view gives some indication of the general downpour. *Continued overleaf*

From previous page
The huge crowds waiting patiently in Victoria Square (facing page, top) were entertained by the band of the Loyal Regiment and by a last minute vacuuming of the red carpet on the Town Hall steps.

Cheering reached a crescendo as the royal car drew up and the Queen gave a special smile to the 12 members of the Bolton branch of the British Limbless Ex-Servicemen's Association, who were seated near the Town Hall steps (facing page,

bottom). The royal standard was unfurled as the royal couple inspected the Guard of Honour and entered the Town Hall. Both Queen Elizabeth and Prince Philip were impressed by the beauty of the Civic Centre and were interested by the various pieces of silver which had been presented to the Albert Hall by leading local industrialists.

The royal party left the Town Hall at precisely 10.23am. The photograph gives some idea of the pomp and ceremony of the occasion as the Queen and the Mayor descend the steps of the special dais. No doubt the uniforms and saluting stirred memories in the hearts of the seated ex-servicemen, proudly displaying their medals. The Queen wore a turquoise outfit, but what was most appropriate was the diamond and pearl badge of the Loyal Regiment in her lapel. This had been presented to her in 1953 when she had become Colonel-in-Chief of the regiment. It was men of the Loyals and the King's Own who, with bayonets fixed, lined Great Moor Street, Newport Street and Victoria Square. The fleet of grand cars departing from the Town Hall is featured in the final photograph, one which also gives some sense of the atmosphere of the occasion. The cheering crowds in Victoria Square are dense, up to 10 deep and people have scrambled on to every vantage point simply to catch a glimpse of the royal couple. This captures the spirit of the day. The citizens of Bolton were not going to let a drop of rain deter them from showing their patriotism and enjoying a bit of pageantry. The children were especially thrilled, for this was an age that was largely innocent of television and royalty had to be seen in person or not at all. To the accompaniment of the bells of St Peter's Church, the royal cavalcade departed via Deansgate and Churchgate. Close watchers noticed that Lord Derby did not observe the family tradition of drawing down the blinds of his car when it passed Churchgate Cross, the site of the execution of his illustrious ancestor in 1651. This was just one of the many little fragments which, when put together, made up a memorable day for the people of Bolton.

On the move

Above: An all too familiar sight today - the dreaded roadworks - but this photograph dates back to 1951 when the volume of traffic was much lighter and roadworks were a relative rarity. Nevertheless, the Chorley New Road scheme was considered a necessity and for its day it was a big undertaking. Work had been in progress since 1948, involving the reconstruction of almost three miles of road at a cost of £160,000. At a ceremony which marked the completion of the scheme, on May 31st 1951, it was commented that the road had been built initially for the carriages of Bolton cotton magnates and had never been intended for heavy traffic. Somewhat controversially, the road surface was concrete and this was the 'brainchild' of the Borough Engineer of the time, Charles Herbert. He had been impressed by the concrete German 'autobahns', although it was stressed that this new surface was experimental. Little did anyone know at this opening ceremony just how much the future lay in concrete in terms of road-building, or that Chorley New Road would eventually be superseded as the main route by the M61. The picture shows the scheme near completion, along with one piece of pure nostalgia - the fine old British Road Services Wagon.

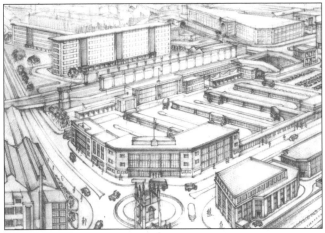

Above: 'Planner's dream; public's nightmare'. This represented the view of the majority of Bolton's citizens when, in 1980, Greater Manchester Transport proposed a new bus station at Dawes Street to replace the existing one at Moor Lane. The artist's impression of the finished scheme may have appealed to some, but the proposed cost of around £3 million did not go down well with the Bolton representatives on the Greater Manchester Council. It was not only cost. Those against the new plan argued that Dawes Street was considerably further from the main shopping area, especially Ashburner Street Market, than was Moor Lane. This would put an extra burden on shoppers, particularly the elderly and may adversely affect town centre trade. Greater Manchester Transport argued that the Moor Lane bus station was not big enough, but the reply was that money would be better spent on expanding and upgrading Moor

Lane. The latter had definitely not been a planner's dream. It had begun life in 1930 as a wooden and shelterless platform on a site formerly occupied by Bessemer Steel. Passenger platforms and canopies had only been added in 1969. However, it was the Dawes Street Plan that was rejected and Moor Lane received a £1.5 million refit in 1985.

Top: A glorious collection of vintage pre-war coaches greets the eye in this shot of a busy Moor Street Bus Station in July 1939. Bolton Holiday Week is in full swing and for those not going away on holiday a wonderful selection of day-trips is on offer from both Ribble and Arthur Christy. The latter is offering a variety of destinations, whilst Ribble seems to be concentrating on those old favourites, Blackpool and Morecambe, at prices ranging from five shillings (25p) to six shillings and three pence (31p). For the real stay-at-homes, the noise and colour of the fair, pictured in the background, would have tempted many to dispose of some of that hard-earned holiday pay. Such was the all-pervading nature of holiday week that stories of Bolton folk on holiday filled the 'Bolton Evening News' in July 1939. A new luxury holiday camp at Prestatyn was benefiting from 600 holiday-makers from Bolton. Rhyl was seemingly 50 percent 'Bolton' and according to a local amusement caterer, Bolton folk were 'good spenders'. Light-hearted stories from the resorts, however, could not mask the headline news of sombre events in Europe that were pushing the country closer to war in July 1939.

Shopping spree

IN 1949 IT WAS REPORTED THAT A LARGE NUMBER OF BOLTON FOLK WERE OFF TO THE SEASIDE FOR CHRISTMAS

December 1949 and the hustle and bustle of Deansgate gives every appearance of the frantic rush to get home early or to get some last minute shopping done. There are plenty of vintage cars here to delight the eye of the connoisseur, but the floods of people crossing the road seem to be paying little heed to the traffic. The number of headscarves on view is typical of this era, but the amount of trilbies as opposed to flat hats seems to suggest that shopping on Deansgate was an occasion for getting 'donned up'. The volume and variety of goods in modern-day stores would have seemed amazing to these 1949 shoppers, for ration books still lingered on in this age of post-war austerity. Nevertheless, Christmas was approaching and in the run-up to the festive season of 1949, it was reported that Santa's Grotto at a 'large concern in the town centre' had 40,000 visitors. Also, bus conductors tried to capture that Christmas spirit by wearing sprigs of holly or mistletoe in their caps. Perhaps surprisingly for the time, it was also reported that a number of Bolton people were off to the seaside for Christmas, with Blackpool the most popular choice.

Below: A sad story of closed pubs is one theme of this early 1960s view of Churchgate looking towards the tall tower of the Parish Church. The two public houses on the right both had a Derby connection. The Cornbrook Ales sign belonged to the Derby Arms. The link of the Legs of Man Hotel with the Derby family was that historically the family provided governors to the Isle of Man. The entire block of buildings was demolished in the 1960s to make way for new office blocks, including the one which houses the 'Bolton Evening News'. Pubs had clearly become an endangered species at this end of Churchgate, although the Boar's Head, to the left, hung on until 1992. It was demolished in 1997, but is soon to be rebuilt. The low white building nearest the camera on the left, is Walsh's famous Pastie Shop, still going strong today. This building has been in existence since at least 1667 and parts of the interior are considerably older. Just beyond the Boar's Head was Church House Garage. This contained a huge turntable for cars which came in for petrol. The varied traffic on Churchgate includes an increasingly rare sight by the 1960s - a horse and cart.

Bolton Evening News

Above: Victoria Square was named after Queen Victoria to celebrate her Diamond Jubilee in 1897. Both before and since, it has undergone many changes in both appearance and function. By around 1824 the market had moved here from Churchgate and it was popularly known as the 'pot market' In 1855 the market took another move, this time to the new Market Hall at Knowsley Street. With the advent of the age of the bus, Victoria Square became the principal bus terminus for Bolton until Moor Lane Bus Station came into being in 1930. This picture was taken in 1954 and about the only feature remaining unaltered now is the impressive War Memorial, although some splendid cast iron work by the local Hick family was removed to make way for it. This consisted of a gas lamp, a circular horse trough and a public drinking fountain. The War Memorial was unveiled in July 1928 by the Earl of Derby and the bronze figures on either side were added in 1933. The group on the left symbolises 'Struggle' and on the right we have 'Sacrifice' with 'Peace'. The fine array of 1950s cars, including that old favourite the Ford Popular, would not now be tolerated along the pedestrianised Precinct.

This just has to be a Saturday afternoon on a Deansgate which is absolutely 'choc-a-bloc' with shoppers. Two opposing floods of people appear to be on a collision course as the red lights hold the traffic up in this photograph from the 1950s. For those who can make it, the pleasures of Littlewoods and 'Woolies' await, but if this is the scene outside the stores, the mayhem inside does not bear thinking about. Both sites for these stores had interesting backgrounds. Littlewoods was built where the Old Embassy Cinema used to stand, the last performance here being in 1947. This branch of Woolworth and Co Ltd opened in 1926. The building was known as Britannia House, once the home of Constantine Bros, drapers and funeral furnishers. A very fine and large statue of Britannia stood on the top of this building until its removal in 1942. Possibly it was thought that this local landmark might well serve the same purpose for enemy aircraft. In 1959, not long after this photograph was taken, Woolworth was rebuilt and extended. Littlewoods was replaced by Halfords in 1967.

It's a bright but brisk day on Newport Street, probably around the middle of the 1950s. Hats and topcoats are the order of the day and the toddler passing Timpson is certainly well clad. An examination of the shop names reveals that Timpson have 'two bites of the cherry', as well as offering a shoe repair service above the premises next to the Corset Shop. This is a rather quaint name for a product that even then was more likely to be called a 'foundation garment'. Nowadays an equivalent shop is likely to sell 'lingerie'. Other names on Newport Street which might jog a few memories

are Salisburys, True-Form, Price's, Greenhalgh's, Dewhurst, Blowers and Cavendish. A Morris Minor can be seen on the far left of the photograph, where Newport Street joins Victoria Square. The fine and prominent building which housed the old Lending Library makes its presence felt on this corner. It is now a branch of the Nationwide Building Society. The grand old Commercial Hotel is just visible in Victoria Square. Over forty years on, this part of Newport Street presents a very different picture. In 1969 it became part of the pedestrianised Precinct, along with Victoria Square and Oxford Street.

It would have been as difficult for local residents in 1800 to picture this scene as it is for us to imagine it as it then was - pleasant meadow land containing an orchard. This is Victoria Square in April 1961 and the whole scenario sums up the traffic problem which had become acute by this date. Rising prosperity and the mass production of relatively cheap family cars were bringing the pleasures of motoring within the reach of thousands of ordinary households. Along with the pleasure, however, came the pain - congestion in town centres and traffic jams. 'Road rage' may be a phrase of the 1990s, but there was plenty of it about in the 1960s. Another hazard, this time mainly to pedestrians, was the constant haze of traffic fumes, especially at a time when all petrol was leaded. Therefore the creation of pedestrian precincts and large car parks was a feature of many urban plans from the 1960s. This formed the background for the creation of 'The Precinct' by Bolton Planning Department, a pedestrianisation scheme which has won several awards. A pleasant shopping stroll in the modern 'Precinct' certainly has the edge over the traffic-dodging experience of 1961.

At work

Both pages: 'Washday Blues', might be the main memory evoked in the minds of older readers at the sight of these three pictures, unless they were lucky enough to enjoy the services of the Bolton Co-operative Laundry. The date of the photographs is around 1937-38, well before the time of washing-machines becoming a common household item. Washday (usually a Monday) for many housewives was a day of drudgery with the posser, the washboard and the mangle. Not only this, women with large families and poor incomes would often take on other people's washing as well, to earn a few extra pence.

For those who could afford it, however, there was always the option of the laundry, with delivery to and from the door. In the case of this photograph, the delivery man was a Mr Joe Kay, who ran a snack bar in the Market Hall after the war. By all accounts Joe was a cheerful chap, easily identifiable at a distance through his theme tune of 'Miss Annabelle Lee'.

The Co-operative Society at this time was an immensely strong and popular organisation which acted almost like a mini Welfare State, offering services from 'the cradle to the grave'. Your first baby clothes might be bought at the Co-op and you might be finally laid to rest by its

funeral services. In between came such things as the Co-operative Laundry Service and the second photograph shows Joe and companion at the Deane Road depot. The two vehicles were spanking new electric delivery vans. The transport foreman, 'Yab' Bridge, standing on his right, looks suitably proud of his new acquisitions. They were for use specifically in the Deane and Morris Green areas. What a distinctive sight they must have been, along with the distinctive sound of 'Miss Annabelle Lee' competing with the whine of an electric motor.

Inside the laundry we are back to a touch of drudgery and a rather poignant story.

The photograph above gives some impression of all the heat and steam engendered in the collar department, as elsewhere in the laundry. Machinery would do the bulk of the work, but it is likely that those collars would have to be ironed by hand. Who would regret the passing of the separate shirt collar?

The supposed advantage was that you did not need to change your shirt daily, only the collar. The great disadvantage was having your neck imprisoned in a noose of unyielding, starched material, that is if you could win the wrestling match with the infernal collar stud. It is known that the lady dealing with the collars at the Co-operative Laundry was Ivy Scott. No doubt she did her share of ironing and starching, but the poignancy of the picture lies in the fact that a few years later, during the war, both Ivy and her baby were to die from a gas leak at their home in Salisbury Street.

Providing vital components for sixty years

Bellhouse Hartwell & Co, now a member of the Hampson Industries Group, is renowned today for the provision of specialised components to the Aerospace industry. 1998 saw the Company celebrating its 60th birthday and a history that embraces a broad spectrum of manufacture including, fire engines, dummy bombs, touring coaches - even pots and pans!

The company was established under its familiar name back in 1938, as an offshoot of Bellhouse Higson Textiles. Bellhouse Higson had been involved in the textile industry since the end of the 19th century, but by the 1930s found itself in circumstances that suggested an expansion into engineering would offer attractive benefits.

At that time, Westhoughton - where the company is still based - was deemed to be one of the most depressed areas of the country. Unemployment was high, business activity sluggish, to put it mildly, and an atmosphere of gritty retrenchment pervaded local commerce. Bellhouse Higson were swimming forcefully against the tide when they set about generating their own good fortune, refusing to dig in until conditions improved. A move into engineering represented a mere taster, however, of what was soon to emerge as a bold policy of development into new fields - as it turned out, this was to be a sure-fire route to commercial success at a time when many other companies were going to the wall. The big idea that saw the establishment of an entirely new concern, Bellhouse Hartwell & Co, came in the form of a dynamic shift into coachbuilding. The works and personnel were ideally placed to develop this new sphere of production, and under new management designs were soon put in hand. Suddenly, there was a climate of excitement in an area where there had been so much doom and gloom, and an invigorated workforce rose enthusiastically to meet the fresh challenge.

Prototypes of the new vehicles were built on site at the Green Vale Works and by 1938 had been thoroughly tested. But just as the company was on the brink of production, world events intervened. The phoney war, as tensions rose inexorably throughout Europe, saw a dramatic process of rearmament in

Great Britain, and a spiralling demand for materials and products that Bellhouse Hartwell were able to provide - specifically, aircraft components. Plans for coach manufacture were temporarily shelved (although investment already made in this area was to reap lucrative benefits soon after the war) and the works switched to building aircraft and aircraft components in conjunction with AVRO of Manchester. (AVRO is known thesedays as British Aerospace Regional Aircraft or BARA).

Wartime was a tremendously busy period at Bellhouse Hartwell. The Air Ministry was a voracious customer, and the company was obliged to tackle an exceptionally wide range of product manufacture, in particular for Spitfire and Lancaster aeroplanes, with a diminishing workforce. (In common with most other industries, as more and more men were conscripted or joined up, women were increasingly called upon to step into their shoes; Bellhouse Hartwell employed a good many as riveters and welders.) Experience gained at this time was to prove invaluable later on when the company committed itself exclusively to the aerospace industry, but a commitment to coachbuilding, and a profound optimism about its future potential, saw little time wasted by the firm, even during the war, in capitalising on opportunities in this area. So it was that Bellhouse Hartwell took an order from the Navy, Army, Air Force Institute, better known as NAAFI, for the supply of 50 mobile canteens.

It is not known how the original order came about - but Bellhouse Hartwell's undoubted skills

Below: One of the Fordson mobile canteens built by Bellhouse Hartwell for the NAAFI at the onset of the Second World War.

in precision engineering, combined with a flexible and enthusiastic readiness to apply their talents to fresh challenges both played their part.

During the war the British people demonstrated remarkable reserves of tenacity and improvisation - making do with little and transforming what they had into vital resources for the war effort. Everywhere, new uses were found for the old and familiar - majestic country houses were commandeered as military bases and hospitals, iron railings plucked from the pavements of urban streets to fashion munitions, lovingly-tended flower gardens brutally cleared and given over to the humble, but nourishing, potato and other crops. So it was that pre-war vehicles, in particular vans, were converted - by Bellhouse Hartwell and others - into mobile refreshment providers, both for the armed forces and for the emergency services and civilian population at times of trouble in our bomb-blasted towns and cities.

NAAFI served the armed forces worldwide, looking after the human, personal needs of military personnel as they battled for their country, boosting morale - a vital wartime task - through, for example, food distribution and the coordination of mail deliveries (a role they still perform today). New chassis were unavailable for their much-needed refreshment vans and, instead, various donors were enlisted to help fund the conversion of existing vehicles. Bellhouse Hartwell fell to the task with enthusiasm, incorporating imaginative touches in the final product - including side screens at the counter opening to provide welcome protection from the weather for the volunteer staff inside!

When the war came to an end, the experience gained in mobile canteen production was to prove its weight in gold - encouraging confidence in local coach operators who swiftly began to place orders with the company for new vehicles. In 1946 the first coach bodies bearing the name of Bellhouse Hartwell appeared. Built for Smith's of Wigan, they were constructed on a Leyland PS1 Chassis, and provided luxury accommodation for long journeys. In fact, it was to be the first of Smith's post-war fleet to embark on Continental tours. Spencer's Tours of Manchester became another early customer and more operators quickly followed.

Coach bodies built by Bellhouse Hartwell at this time were of composite construction - although a high proportion of steel was already a feature, even at this introductory stage, to provide

Above: Drop tanks being manufactured in the late 1940s.

additional strength. The design proved successful, and popular, but with the advent of the underfloor engine chassis (a postwar development), Bellhouse Hartwell identified the need for a body of even greater durability - particularly in order to meet the demands of very large service mileages, which were beginning to be envisaged. So it was that a further period of design and development followed -

lasting two years and culminating in the production of an applauded all-metal body which became the foundation for an attractive range of coaches for a broad spectrum of customers. A notable example was the 'Landmaster' model. Its main frame was designed to accommodate modification in a number of areas - permitting a wide range of external finishes and internal specifications - and offered luxury seating for up to 41 passengers. The Mark III version, developed especially for Blue Cars (Continental) Ltd, resulted in 18 new coaches for long distance

travel with many innovative features. Constructed on a Leyland 'Royal Tiger' chassis, and measuring 30 feet by 8 feet over all, this model had an all steel body frame and combined maximum strength with minimal weight (both highly desirable in a commercial vehicle). Curved wing mouldings enabled an attractive dual colour scheme on the exterior, while the interior was sumptuously appointed with 32 armchair seats, upholstered in specially woven plain blue pile cloth. With hot, foreign climates in mind, each passenger was supplied with an individual cool air supply - entirely familiar today, but in the 1950s thought to be unique to aircraft. Another bright idea seems to have been the provision of loose hassocks (plastic covered) which were considered to be 'a boon and a

Above: One of six Bellhouse Hartwell Mark II "Landmasters" operated by Scout Motor Services of Preston. Below: The premises pictured in the 1960s.

Above: VC10 Engine door repair activities.

blessing to passengers of less then average height'! The particular requirements of individual operators were effortlessly served by all the 'Lancaster' coaches - and customers included Scout Motor Coaches, Transglobe Tours, Melba Tours of Stockport and Knowles of Bolton. The 'Monarch' class of coach, meanwhile, designed to suit a forward control chassis, found similar success with Embankment Motors of Plymouth and Newquay Motors, among others.

The emphasis on all metal construction, coupled with a surplus of the material generally, gave Bellhouse Hartwell inspiration for a foray into something entirely new. Armed with a recently acquired quantity of surplus aluminium, the Company embarked on the manufacture of domestic items, such as pots and pans, under the name of Bellso Ware. So popular did this sideline become that 'Bellso' was generally assumed to have inspired the phrase 'sound as a bell'! (Not so, of course - Shakespeare was already using the term - 'He hath a heart as sound as a bell, and his tongue is the clapper' - in his play 'Much Ado About Nothing' in 1598!). Domestic manufacture was really never more than an interesting diversion for Bellhouse Hartwell, but it provided a welcome inflow of funds during a time of substantial investment for the firm, and demonstrates, yet again, a characteristic adroitness in seizing opportunities which has done much over the years to ensure a dynamic reputation for which the company is still celebrated. Coachbuilding also provided its own opportunities, typified in the early 1950s by a specialised assignment - the construction of two fire engines for local brigades.

At this period, an aircraft called the Canberra was being built in Preston and Salmesbury. When the Korean War threatened and then broke, the government placed an order for 1000 of these aeroplanes to be manufactured. The British Aircraft Corporation (a conglomeration of major aircraft companies) took on the project but were unable to complete it without subcontracting some of the tasks. Bellhouse Hartwell, always on hand in such situations, quickly won the contract to manufacture the Canberra's wing tip fuel tanks - a lucrative order which saw the firm taking on many extra staff, and a dramatic increase in overtime working. It was also to herald the dawn of Bellhouse Hartwell's modern incarnation as a specialised aircraft component manufacturer.

Similar contracts followed over the next two decades: the firm made long range fuel tanks for special missions undertaken by Canberra, and was closely involved in the Avro 748 project (the 'penny a mile' aircraft), which saw a nice convergence of its passenger service and aircraft component expertise - Bellhouse Hartwell provided the aeroplane's hat racks, cockpit furniture including centre and side consoles complete with wiring and engraving in three

languages, and passenger service units. British Aircraft Corporation work included fuel tanks, access ladders, rocket packs and reconnaissance packs for the Lightning project.

In 1970 the company was bought by Hampson Industries, which secured its long term future, although the 1970s were for Bellhouse Hartwell - as for many other firms - a lean decade in terms of trade. Lean pickings in the aircraft manufacturing industry saw a contracting workforce, but new challenges for those who remained. A notable project from this era was the manufacture of a dummy bomb, which will forever be remembered as the Hartwell bomb.

When economic conditions improved, the business was soon prospering again. British Aerospace started to provide many more orders, including one for Jaguar air intakes, alongside work on the Canberra refurbishment programme and various others. Before long, Greengate and Woodford looked to Bellhouse Hartwell when updating VC10 and Nimrod aircraft.

Below: Avro regional jet components being assembled for the RJ85 and RJ100 programme in May 1998.

The modern age dawned and expansion at the company found a formal structure and substantial investment. In 1989, a satellite company - BHW Components - was established on a greenfield site in Wigan and in 1992 the Bellhouse Hartwell Aerospace Group of companies came into being.

Today the Group consists of two companies employing 600 people with plans for further growth through acquisition high on the agenda. Bellhouse Hartwell & Co has an unrivalled reputation in its field, gaining the MAD Military Aircraft Division Bronze Award for the Preferred Supplier Process and the group is currently making strides towards the coveted silver award on the new BAe Plc. Supplier Excellence Process (SEP).

There are three main areas to the Company's focus of work: sheet metal detail manufacture, sub-assembly of airframe components and repair and overhaul facilities for civil and military aircraft structures. Focusing on these core services, the name of Bellhouse Aerospace Group has become well known for the provision of complete support packages which is underpinned by a 'One Stop Shop' capability, project management and manufacturing resource with a quality and delivery service second to none. Counting many of the aerospace industry's major names amongst its customer list, British Aerospace, Shorts, GKN Westlands and Rolls Royce all included, Bellhouse Aerospace Group is certainly a force to be reckoned with.

Along with its parent company, Hampson Industries Plc., it has invested in further activities such as anodising, production tooling, chemi-mill, seam welding, stretchforming, CNC pipe bending, drop hammer, x-ray facilities together with computer aided design facilities including CADDS 5 and CATIA solid modelling techniques, which will ensure the Group is well positioned in the market place with the opportunity to extend its core skills towards the goal of 'World Class Best Cost Producer'.

A far cry from mobile canteens perhaps, but Bellhouse Hartwell's contemporary role is still discernibly in the mould created over 60 years ago at its inception: to be there when it matters, with the best.

Above: The premises as they are in the 1990s.

A unique blend of modern luxury, natural beauty and olde worlde charm

On a picturesque spot some four miles north of Bolton, on the fringe of open moorland with panoramic views over the surrounding countryside, stands the Last Drop Village and Hotel. This unique hotel and leisure centre occupies a site which has been inhabited since the early eighteenth century, when a cluster of farm buildings grew up here. Contemporary records refer to those dwellings as Orrell Fold, and it is believed that the Orrell family who resided here were descendants of the Orrells who held the manor of Turton from the time of John de Tarbock's death, around 1420, until 1628. William Orrell was the first of the family to become Lord of the Manor, and the title was handed down through the generations for over two centuries. The tower and its Rights were finally sold to Humphrey Chetham in 1628, and the Chethams remained Lords of Turton until the nineteenth century.

The next record of the Orrell family shows John Orrell as tenant of Orrell Fold in the early part of the eighteenth century. In 1748 he was appointed Trustee of a neighbouring farm at Goose Cote Hill, which had been bequested by Humphrey Chetham for the benefit of the poor; this meant that revenue from the farm was used to buy clothes for the poor

and needy. This building then became the Turton Workhouse, where the poor of Turton were set to work at tasks such as handloom weaving. Each town used to hire persons to hold Parish Offices, and the various parish responsibilities such as overseeing the poor as Beadle, and overseeing the highways, would be distributed amongst the incumbents. John Orrell was officially hired to hold Parish Offices in 1763, although as Trustee of the Workhouse he would already have been involved in helping the poor. He died in 1778, leaving Orrell Fold to his eldest son, Isaac, who took over the running of the farm. At that time there were three

This picture and above: *Two views of the derelict Orrell Fold pictured shortly before Mr Carton Walker purchased the farm.*

principal farmers, and it is likely that there were additional tenants living in the adjoining cottages. Isaac's brothers also continued living at Orrell Fold, and when Isaac died in 1822 and his sons had no interest in the farm, it passed to his nephew Samuel Orrell, a Yeoman.

By the 1820s mills were starting up in the area, and as the mills increased in number and began to dominate the marketplace, the small cottage industries were driven almost out of existence. As industrialisation continued to spread, small self-sufficient areas such as Orrell Fold found it increasingly difficult to survive. Most of the land at Orrell Fold was meadow or pasture; oats and potatoes were grown, and one of the cottages served as a shop. The census of 1841 records 42 people living there, amongst whom were farmers, agricultural labourers, weavers, stonemasons, cotton workers and quarrymen. By 1871, the number of occupants had fallen to 16, and several buildings were now left unoccupied. Samuel Orrell had left the farm by this time, having moved to Atherton with his family in the late 1860s; a few other members of the family may have remained there for a time, but the long line of Orrells in Turton was at an end.

Around the turn of the century, quarrying took place at Orrell Fold; the land extended across Hospital Road and as far west as Darwen Road, and was occupied by John James Crooke, who sold the farm in 1911 to

Eli Stanford. The farm changed hands again in 1920 when it was sold to William and Thomas Oddie, but it seems that some misunderstanding arose in the course of the transaction, as a result of which the Stanford family moved out of the main farmhouse but were allowed to live in the adjoining cottage rent free until they purchased another farm two years later. The Oddie brothers occupied the main farmhouse; William subsequently married and moved into the cottage which is now the Tea Shop, and around 1930 the Oddies sold Orrell Fold to Mr William Carr, a well-known farmer and racehorse owner who lived on a farm in the Dunscar area of Bolton. Orrell Farm was used mainly for stabling and exercising Mr Carr's horses, and the buildings, left largely unoccupied, fell into neglect. It is recorded that a Mr Eli Stanford, grandson of the former owner, who had lived at Orrell Fold with his grandfather from 1914 to 1920, paid a return visit to the farm in the early 1960s; horses were still stabled there, but he was saddened to see the buildings in a state of dereliction. It was shortly after this visit, however, that Mr Carr sold the farm to Mr Carton Walker, the son of a well-known local family who owned a large tannery business in Bolton.

Carton Walker saw that the natural beauty of the location and the charm of the remaining buildings gave the site tremendous potential as the setting for an exclusive restaurant, and devised plans to convert the derelict buildings without destroying their original character. The shippon became the restaurant; the old stone cow stalls were

Top left: An aerial view of the Last Drop Village during a May Bank Holiday Fair during the 1980s. Centre: The Last Drop sign that hangs outside the hotel entrance. Right: The Drop Inn Pub and entrance to the Stocks Restaurant.

courtyard, in the centre of which is a sheltered lawn with a fountain and a dovecote. Running round the courtyard is a two-storey building with a wooden balcony, housing well-equipped hotel bedrooms; there is further accommodation for guests in the central block with its distinctive Clock Tower, in Orrell Cottage, which is one of the original farm buildings, and in other village buildings. In the village the Drop Inn Pub, with ivy covered walls and mullioned windows, occupies the lower half of the barn; next to it stands Stocks Restaurant which serves good food in an informal atmosphere, and next to that, constructed from the remains of the old barn with a traditional tithe barn beamed roof, is the Penny Farthing Suite, which provides conference, exhibition and private function facilities. Along High Street and in the Market Place are a complete

retained, and cartwheels were covered with glass to become tables, each lit by an old miner's lamp. The roof is open-timbered, the air is kept circulating by a

large wooden aircraft propeller, and there is a fascinating collection of antiques; the overall result is an intimate dining area where diners can enjoy a memorable evening. Next to the restaurant is the cocktail bar, which looks out across the whole of the Bolton and Winter Hill area, and used to be a farm midden. Again, there are many antiques to intrigue and amuse guests, including a beautifully preserved Brougham which contains a public telephone.

A small cobbled passage with Georgian bow windows leads from the cocktail bar to the hotel

range of village shops including the Tea Shop, the Village Bakery and various craft shops where visitors can watch craftsmen at work. At the end of High Street, the North-West Tourist Board has its headquarters in Rosehill Cottage, which also houses the luxurious Lancaster Suite, comprising bedroom and panelled lounge, and the Turton Suite which is available for special functions; functions can also be held in the large

Top Left: A charming summer view of the Village High Street. *Above:* The Hotel and Reception Block. *Below:* An artists impression of the whole complex.

Pennine Suite, the split-level Mimosa Room on the ground floor of the Hotel, and the smaller Chetham Room with its wood panelled walls and oak beamed ceiling. At the edge of the village, a health and club has been built to provide a full range of along facilities to residents and club members.

All this has evolved from Carton Walker's original restaurant. The hotel, craft shop, tea shop and various other additions were implemented by Carton Walker himself. He sold the site in 1978 and the new owners added more bedrooms, shops and the leisure complex. Macdonalds Hotels acquired The Last Drop Village and Hotel in 1996, and the ever-increasing number of visitors has meant that the expansion of the facilities has continued; at present, the hotel has 128 bedrooms, and the Pennine Suite can seat 450 guests for dinner and 700 for theatre style meetings. Yet throughout the programme of conversions and extensions, care has been taken to preserve as many original features as possible and incorporate them into the new developments, making this village truly unique.

There has been much speculation as to the origins of the name of the village. In fact, the Last Drop's name suggested itself to Carton Walker one evening after dinner, when he offered 'the last drop' of wine to the friend with whom he had dined. But whilst we know the origins of the name, and can trace back some of the history of Orrell Fold and its occupants, visitors to the village still experience a tantalising sense of catching a glimpse of a bygone era whose mysteries we can only guess at, whilst being able to relax in the beautiful surroundings and enjoy every modern luxury.

Above: The restaurant pictured soon after opening, note the original animal stalls had been incorporated into the layout. *Below:* 'Bumbles Beestro', pictured in the early 1980s before it became the Tea Shop.

Flying colours

Geoffrey de Havilland was one of the great pioneers of aircraft design and production of the first half of the twentieth century. The private enterprise aeroplane manufacturers of pre-World War One days offered pilot training in the same way that car makers ran courses for chauffeurs. De Havilland bombers played a vital role during that conflict.

In late 1928 two dozen DH9As and ten other aircraft evacuated the Afghan royal household and the entire British diplomatic community from trouble torn Kabul. This classic use of air power occurred in the middle of the inter-war deterioration of aircraft supplies when the services were starved of funding. Better known to the 'air minded' public of the era were the well publicised air races and record flights.

The first de Havilland Comet was a graceful futuristic machine built of wood for the 1934 MacRobertson Air Race between London and Melbourne. She completed the 11,300 miles in seventy two hours. From this classic design was developed the wartime Mosquito nicknamed the 'Wooden Wonder'.

The de Havilland Airscrew Company was set up, by the parent company, in 1936, at the Garside Street Works in Bolton. A year later a new factory was built at Lostock to house nine hundred employees making propellers. The Lostock site had previously hosted Sir Alan Cobham's famous 'National Aviation Days'. Later Jim Mollison's Gypsy Moth, of the Australian record flight, and the Fox Moth which won the 1932 King's Cup Race were shown here. Sir Alan had once walked away from a crash in Ainsworth Lane, Bolton, following a short flight from Lostock.

The Lostock factory was officially opened on 15th July 1938 by Sir Thomas Inskip, Minister for Co-ordination of Defence. By now the nation had woken up to the Nazi menace and by the outbreak of war in September 1939 some ten thousand propellers had been made for twenty aircraft types.

During World War Two Lostock worked night and day producing and repairing propellers and ancillary

Below: The British Aerospace site in May 1957. On the building it says De Havilland Propellers Limited.

equipment. This valuable site was protected by a battery of 4.5 inch anti-aircraft guns located on the left of Alexandra Road, twin Lewis machine guns on the gate house roof and Hispano anti-tank guns in each of the two pill boxes. Additionally smudge pots were located along Chorley New Road which could blanket the entire works with black smoke to frustrate enemy bomb aimers who needed to see their target.

The Home Guard, commanded by Major H Morton, retd, were trained to deal with the incendiary bombs which never came. Although the Luftwaffe had photographed the site in 1941 the nearest bomb damage was opposite the Rumworth Hotel on Wigan Road. Even so a fleet of lorries took vital blade forgings to dispersal units every night of the war to ensure a reserve in case of air raids. The site of today's West Block was then a lorry park for the company's Queen Mary's, these sixty foot aircraft transporters were then the longest vehicles on the road.

Petrol was severely rationed and although cars were rare only a few key workers received petrol coupons. Most people walked, cycled or took the tram to work and ate in the canteen where meat

pie, mash and gravy for a 'tanner', 6d or 2.5p, was the staple offering. Office clerks were paid eighteen shillings, 90p, for a five and a half day week. Production workers, with ample overtime, earned considerably more than this. In 1941 de Havilland laid on their first Family Day with a 'bunfight' and stalls in the canteen.

Above: Inside the factory staff are hard at work in 1961, everyone here is highly focused without being distracted by their photograph being taken.
Below: A close up view of young men building a propeller.

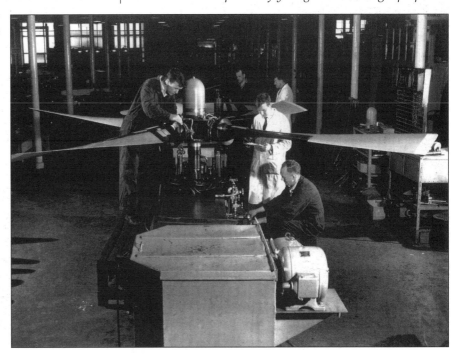

In the early post war years de Havilland, and other British manufacturers, worked all out both to regain pre-war markets and to win new ones. The DH Dove made her first flight on 25 September 1945 followed soon after, on 10 May 1950, by the DH Heron. Both aircraft were propeller driven unlike the revolutionary DH Comet, the world's first commercial jet airliner, which became a market leader for many years. During the heady days of the Berlin Airlift the Repair Department and machinists worked to war- time capacity maintaining the transport aircraft which denied West Berlin to Soviet rule.

Meanwhile in the new West Block modest, almost Heath Robinson, experiments were being made in the new field of electronics. The types D and E Vibrators tested aircraft wings for little known inflight metal fatigue which led to the mysterious disappearances of successful aeroplanes. By 1955 de Havilland was the largest employer in Bolton, benefiting the town with its £50,000 weekly wages bill and by the sixties Lostock had the largest machine shop in Europe. In 1961 the electronics experiments paid off when the RAF took delivery of the DH Firestreak guided missile.
Later, components were made for the Blue Streak satellite launcher rocket.

Lostock built propellers continued to play a vital part in aeronautical development. In Operation 'Over Basseua' static aircraft were positioned to assess the effects, on equipment at varied distances, of the Christmas Island atom bomb explosions. Lostock also ensured that the Short flying boats were equipped to participate in the attempted rescue of the sunk HM Submarine 'Truculent'. Following the Agadir earthquake both the DH Dove and DH Heron light aircraft were invaluable in taking supplies to local runways too damaged to support heavy freighters.

Lostock then diversified into the manufacture of air conditioning for pressured aircraft cabins. The skilled staff turned to making mining and shoe making machinery, components for vending machines and Pottermeters to measure liquid flow in pipelines, aswell as aircraft under-carriages, infra red equipment, motor car engine blocks and cigarette packing and inspection equipment. When the Lostock Supervisory Staff Association - established to forge links with a wide spectrum of commercial concerns - held an Annual Dinner, one guest speaker, a visitor from the National Coal Board, memorably exclaimed: 'If making space rockets and shoemaking machinery isn't playing both ends safe, I'll plait sawdust!'

Between 1937 and 1960 the Lostock branch was known as

Above: The factory floor covered with machinery in 1961, how noisy it must have been for these workers! **Left:** *View of Hawker Siddeley Dynamics Lostock factory at Horwich, near Bolton, which is equipped with 1200 precision machine tools.*

De Havilland Airscrews, except for a period during the war when it was known as DH Propellers. From 1960 to 1963 it was integrated into the De Havilland Aircraft Co, before coming under the umbrella of Hawker Siddeley Dynamics. In 1977 British Aerospace was formed by way of a merger of British Aircraft Corporation, Hawker Siddeley Aviation, Hawker Siddeley Dynamics and Scottish Aviation. This nationalised corporation survived for four years before becoming a public limited company in 1981. The company retained a clear identity throughout 50 years of complex ownership, and name changes - more particularly, the Lostock operation developed an impregnable reputation which was to stand it in excellent stead in 1989, when British Aerospace PLC became a management organisation controlling wholly owned subsidiaries. Subsequently, it was decided, these subsidiary companies should market their own specialised products, under their own names. So it was that Lostock became the Manufacturing Centre for the British Aerospace Dynamics Centre.

A decade of dramatic change followed as the company's workforce united behind a plan to concentrate activities on the production of guided weapons systems. To this end, all aspects of the business were overhauled - management structures redefined, motivational strategies improved, administrative systems revolutionised and a radical change in manufacturing philosophy adopted. The goal was to be world class, and a world-beater. Through an insistence that the company's people constituted its most valuable asset, and that team work and frank communication were essential at every stage, a dramatic transformation was effected at the works.

A world class player now, the company went into partnership in 1996 with Matra Défense of France. Under its new name, Matra BAe Dynamics, the company incorporates almost half of the French and a majority of the British missile industries. A high technology product range with application potential in all battle scenarios - on land, at sea and in the air - now attracts customers from over forty countries in five continents. With a turnover in excess of £1 billion it has become Europe's number one guided weapons business.

A world beater? No doubt about it. But the testing standards and success already achieved have done little to stifle the undoubted enthusiasm within the company to go even further. In the words of Steve Debonnaire, General Manager of Lostock and Head of AIT UK: 'It is not just a question of sustaining the standards we have achieved now. We want to improve on them. World class is a never-ending concept'.

Above: Machine shop, the Alarm product line went into production in 1989.
Left: Matra BAe Lostock today, still going strong.

Paper production for over a century and a half

Springside Mill was first established as a paper mill in 1834 by Mr John Livesey. Prior to starting Springside Mill John Livesey had been a partner in another paper mill, but had lost his share in that mill as a result of a dispute with his partner. Unfortunately for Mr Livesey, his new venture did not succeed, and within a short time Springside Mill closed. It was reopened in 1839 by Mr Robert Orrell in conjunction with Mr William Spencer and a partner, Mr Charles Turner. It was Charles Turner's good business acumen which took the mill from strength to strength, and when he died, in 1870, Springside Mill was a well-established, financially secure business. After his death his nephew, Mr Henry Clemson, joined William Spencer in running the business. William Spencer died in 1886 and his son, Robert Orrelle Spencer, became sole proprietor of Springside Mill. The Spencer family were to own the mill until 1969.

When Robert Orrelle Spencer took over, the mill consisted of one paper machine which made brown wrapping and casing paper for the expanding Lancashire textile spinning, weaving and bleaching trades. Production is believed to have been about 18 tons a week, although we have no detailed records. The raw material for the paper making process was jute bagging, manilla rope, flax waste and rags. These materials were placed in large revolving kiers, washed and then bleached.
The process involved - as it does to this day - large amounts of water

Above: W. Spencer, the original founder of the company.
Right: A company Wakes Week outing to Blackpool in the early 1920s.

to allow the process of breaking down the raw material into the individual fibres which are its basic constituents. All transport to and from the mill was by horse and cart; it was not until 1942 that petrol driven vehicles became the norm. The power was provided by a 40 foot water wheel driven from the fast-flowing water channelled down the hillside - the name Springside came from the large number of natural springs occurring around the site. The mill also had a steam engine of some 800hp, built by the local engineering company Hick Hargreaves, and supplied by two Lancashire boilers.

In 1990 Robert Orrelle Spencer installed an MG machine approximately 80" wide. This machine produced paper for bags, an area of the paper market which was growing rapidly at the time. Another MG machine was installed in 1902, and a third in 1908, just after Robert Spencer's death in 1907.

It was in 1908 that Springside Mill became a Limited Company, Charles Turner and Co Ltd. Over the next 22 years a considerable amount of capital was spent on improvements, which included: modernising the three paper machines; rebuilding the Fourdrinier machine at No 4 with a 100" wet end, obtained second hand from Durham Paper Mill in West Hartlepool; installion of a new dry end and up-to-date auxillary plant by Bertrams Ltd of Edinburgh; and a new overhead crane which extended from the top shed over the cellar overlooking No 4. This crane was used to lift the 5' diameter rolls of paper up to the conversion area, enabling the company to diversify into glazed papers

In 1969 Charles Turner & Co Ltd was sold to Courtaulds, who used the mill's machinery to develop the wet lay process for making non-woven textiles, but the development was not a success and experiments ceased. The mill continued to manufacture paper products. In 1985 Ivor Samuel, the Managing Director, led a management buy out; then in 1989 the mill was bought by Hazlewoods Foods. At this period tissue products for the janitorial and hospital markets were being manufactured. In 1996 another management buy out put the mill back into the hands of the Samuel family; the present Managing Director, Nigel Samuel, is Ivor Samuel's son.

for waxing, white printing and writing papers, and other high quality bleached papers. The raw materials for these products were 100% wood pulp. Total production by the end of the 1930's stood at 2500 tons per annum, and during some of this time the machine worked 24 hours a day, 6 days a week.

Production of wadding began on the first MG machine in 1948, expanding to a second machine in 1951 and a third machine in 1962.

Springside Mill can now look forward to a secure future, focusing upon the product, the market, and the customer, thus perpetuating its long tradition of papermaking on the site and continuing to employ local people as it has done for over 164 years.

Taken from information supplied by Gordon Hurst and Joan Patterson.

Above: The works in the early 1900s.
Below: Inside the machine house in Coronation year, 1937.

Protecting companies in the North West

Duval Security was founded in 1985 by Barry Duval to provide a wide ranging security service for firms in the Bolton area. The first premises were in Carne House, Bolton, but within a year Duval's moved to College Way. Three year's later the expanding company took over 602 Chorley New Road, Horwich, the former home of Bolton Training group. Since then the demand for security services are such that new branch offices have been opened not only in nearby Wigan and Manchester but even as far afield as Stoke-on-Trent.

Manned Guarding provides the core of Duval's services which include Static Guarding such as those vital Gate and Reception Security personnel who control ingress and outlet of both goods and visitors at works and office buildings. Their Mobile Patrols within sites with large perimeters or multiple buildings are valued as much by large organisations as the more visible floating patrols which maintain frequent checks for companies with different security requirements.

Such patrols are backed by an ad hoc supervision system designed to keep security staff on their toes. Electronic control mechanisms are available for those wishing to have regular monitoring of patrols.

Conditions of service for their well trained staff protecting clients' properties are in line with those required under the Health and Safety at Work Act for permanent employees of the contracting customer.

Clients concerned for the safe keeping of vital keys to buildings, safes, laboratories and high security stores etc are catered for by Duval's Key Holding service. This is another aspect of the firm's ability to enable clients to sleep at night and enjoy weekends and holidays free of care. It also removes the risk to clients' homes and families that arises through keeping business security gear at home.

"RETAILERS CAN HIRE UNIFORMED DUVAL STORE GUARDS AS A VISIBLE DETERRENT TO OPPORTUNIST THIEVES"

Department stores and other retailers can hire uniformed Duval Store Guards as a visible deterrent to opportunist thieves, just like an instore "village bobby". Businesses which require "plain clothes" Store Detectives on watch for the daring, occasionally clever, tactics of the unprincipalled shop lifter are invaluable when such thievery adds nearly twenty percent to national retail costs. This is an unfortunate statistic that will ensure Duval Security is kept very busy well into the next millennium protecting more of the North West than any other security company.

The company that delivers...every time

Beldam Crossley Limited was formed in 1988 by the merger of the Beldam Packing & Rubber Co. Ltd. of Brentford with Henry Crossley (Packings) Ltd. of Bolton. Both companies had long and distinguished records as manufacturers of braided packings and seals prior to the merger.

Beldam Packing & Rubber Co. Ltd was founded in 1876 by Asplan Beldam to manufacture packings for steam engines in ships. From these beginnings the Beldam company developed an extensive product range for maintenance engineers around the world. It became famous for the quality, reliability and availability of its PILOT brand packings and jointings through its worldwide network of distributors together with its comprehensive range of pipeline gaskets.

Henry Crossley (Packings) Ltd. was founded in 1917 by Henry Crossley and in the early 1920s the company moved to the present site which is now the head office and factory (7,800 sq metres) for Beldam Crossley Ltd. The company produced braided packings using traditional solid and seam plait construction until Arthur Crossley (The Founders son) developed a technique for braiding in a CROSS PLAIT style. This was followed by patents being granted in the U.K. and U.S.A and most other braided packing manufacturers around the world now incorporate the CROSS PLAIT style in their ranges. During the early 1960s the Crossley company became one of the pioneers in the manufacturing and machining of PTFE and nylon products and the Bolton factory is still one of the foremost producers of these materials in the U.K.

Beldam Crossley Ltd. now employs approximately 230 people working in the Bolton factory and its U.K. distributor network.

Export sales are managed from head office at Bolton and shipments are despatch all over the world from its large (2,250 sq. mettes) central warehouse. The company provides an enviable service to the marine industry through its distributor network; Customer requirements are co-ordinated through our marine sales office to ensure vital parts etc. are available on time whenever a vessel reaches port.

Over the years the company has developed extensive business in selected countries by supplying "Own Brand" packing and seals to customers. This remains an important part of Beldam Crossley's export business and close co-operation between these customers and our knowledgeable marketing staff has established mutual trust and confidence in growing business in otherwise difficult markets.

Above: The premises in the 1960s. **Left:** *An aerial view of the works taken in the 1990s.*

Simply a better class of service

Thistlethwaites was started in 1924 by Christopher Thistlethwaite, formerly the Head Wages Clerk at Dobson and Barlow. His first venture into business had been the purchase of the village store in Darcy Lever. This was a much more certain proposition in the 1920s than today as few people then owned cars and stay at home house wives shopped several times a week, if not on a daily basis.

Christopher Thistlethwaite made another career change by buying a small motor factors in Burns Street, Bolton. From the start he set out to provide customers with a square deal, competitive prices and, to quote from Thistlethwaite's subsequent advertising, "Simply a better class of service".

Sons John and Chris were involved in the family business from the start until in 1936, after twelve years, Chris left the running of the business in John's hands. The growing prosperity enjoyed by many in the late thirties was turned upside down by the outbreak of World War Two.

Manufacturing enterprises of all kinds were turned over to produce war material, men and women were conscripted into the armed forces for "war work", even children worked in fields and hedgerows to collect vital foodstuffs. As a result, rationing and shortages became the order of the day and Thistlethwaites endured the common problems of quotas and making do. In spite of this the young company kept going.

The night of 9th January 1941 saw the Burns Street premises have a near miss when the café next door was destroyed by a direct hit from a bomb. The war time spirit of "Britain can take it" and "Business as usual" saw Bolton and Thistlethwaites through these dark early years until the tide turned and the slogan became "Britain can dish it out". David, the founder's grandson, a stout admirer of such resilient national characteristics, continued the management of the firm in a similar fashion.

The thrifty slogan of early days, "Never scrap a tyre until we've seen it!", is still maintained today although the common practice elsewhere is to replace any item no matter how slightly worn it is. Thistlethwaite's guarantee to repair any serviceable tyre using the latest hot vulcanising technology. This "welding" of rubber ensures that even "HR", "VR", "ZR", high speed tyres are repaired as good as new and that the repairs are the strongest part

Top right: *The company premises pictured in 1948, and parked outside is the van that David learnt to drive in.*
Left: *Staff vulcanising tyres in 1958, David Thistlethwaite is pictured far left.*

of the tyre making these the safest repairs.

Readers may feel that mechanics, like policemen, are getting younger every day. This is not the case at Thistlethwaites where mature, experienced personnel take charge of the motorists' most expensive possession, after

their house that is. The staff work for a company that values long service employees with twenty or so years of company loyalty to their credit. This expertise is backed by state of the art Hoffman Infra Red wheel balancers and the Bear computerised wheel aligner. Politeness and a smile come as standard, for all motorists, from staff dedicated to keeping the wheels of Bolton turning smoothly and safely.

In 1984 Thistlethwaites celebrated the company's Diamond Jubilee, sixty years success as a family run business in a competitive world. Come the Millennium and it will be seventy six years since Chris Thistlethwaite gave up a secure job to be his own boss.

Now the founders great grandson, Chris, is taking over the reins from his father David and along with their manager Ian is ensuring that this specialist company is continuing to provide an expertise and depth of knowledge in the tyre and exhaust business which is not readily available at the high street chain stores.

Today with the rapid development of tyre and vehicle technology Thistlethwaite's are at the forefront of accurate wheel balancing and vehicle alignment which ensures drivers have a perfect vibration free ride. By investing in the very best equipment they are capable of fitting ultra high performance tyres to expensive alloy wheels with the care and precision expected by the modern motorist.

This attention to detail is followed in every aspect of the business whether repairing tyres, fitting a new exhaust, servicing brakes or the computerised testing of the steering geometry and suspension of a car. All this is backed up with the largest stock of leading brand and economy tyres in the North West to provide the discerning motorist with complete peace of mind.

*Top right: Thistlethwaites pictured in the winter of 1984, their Diamond Jubilee year. **Below:** A recent view of the Company's premises.*

A company founded on cheerful service

James Booth (Bolton) Ltd started out in the early part of the century as coal merchants at a time when every house had a chimney and burnt coal.

Mr James Booth founded the firm, and their original premises were on Willows Lane, Bolton from where they stabled the horses that pulled the coal lorries. Mr Booth himself lived in Randal Street where the company's offices were situated.

Coal Merchants used heart shaped shovels to fill the stiff rope handled sacks with a measured hundredweight. The larger coals preferred by some customers often had to be lifted by hand. Every sack was hefted on to the wagon and then carried on the backs of coalmen. Negotiating dogs, steps and other obstacles to tip the coal through narrow chutes in the pavements into inconveniently placed coal bunkers.

At this time it was very much a family business and James Booths' six children, (three boys and three girls), were all expected to help out at every opportunity.

With the progression of time, Mr Booths' eldest son John worked alongside his father in the business, middle son Charles became a Joiner and Builder, and youngest son James went into the Legal profession, (later becoming a Judge).

On the death of the founder Mr James Booth, son John followed his father in this labour intensive business, where customers trust in the quality and service provided were vital to success. By this time motor vehicles were starting to increase in popularity and the business, while continuing to act as coal merchants, additionally now did some tipper haulage for the local traders, particularly builders.

During the war the company's lorries were commandeered to help with war work, such as building airfields. As drivers received their call up papers, old men and horses were called out of retirement to keep

the home fires burning. At war's end and for several years after, it was impossible to replace the worn out vehicles and 'Old faithfuls' had to be patched together and kept going with a mixture of ingenuity and whatever came to hand.

The strain of keeping a business going under such circumstances took it's toll on John Booth and in 1947 the family coal business was sold. The firm now concentrated on the haulage side of the business operating a fleet of twenty, 3 and 5 tonne tipper lorries.

Mr John Booth died prematurely in 1949. His death started a difficult period for the firm, which was starved of money as a result of death duties. John's

Above: One of the very first tipper wagons the Company owned. Below: A very early, one horse powered, coal delivery wagon, pictured at an agricultural show.

wife Phyllis Booth came into the business and was helped by his two brothers Charles and James Booth.

This situation continued for a few years until Phyllis felt able to manage on her own assisted by Mr Burt Livsey who was appointed transport manager.

John and Phyllis's son Barrie joined the company in 1951, then aged 15 years, and was involved in both working in the garage and driving the vehicles.

The company continued with tipper vehicles slowly increasing in size until in the early sixties each vehicles average carrying capacity had grown from 3 to 10 tonnes, with some as much as 20 tonnes.

'Other times, other methods' applies as much to go ahead family businesses as to any other.

John's son Barrie, who now runs the company, has proven to be another Booth ready to contribute to the continuing development of the family firm. Throughout its changing history, Booth's has remained constant in its use of heavy haulage vehicles, often pioneering new developments in this area.

In 1972, the firm bought their first skip loader vehicle and 20 skips diversifying into the waste business. Four years later in 1976 the company acquired Harwood Quarry from which high quality brick shale was dug out for sale to brickmakers.

By 1978 the fleet had expanded to include the first rear end loaders in the North West capable of moving ten skips a day and at the same time, the company

outgrew the premises at Willows Lane and moved to a new 3 acre site at Westhoughton.

Eight years later Booth's had another first: front end loaders which could handle a magnificent forty skips each day. This well developed waste collection side of the enterprise was sold in 1989 to the construction and land fill giants Wimpey Waste Management, who lease part of Booth's Manchester Road site at Westhoughton.

James Booth (Bolton) Ltd currently operate some twenty bulk tippers which carry road salt, finest screed ash and coal, in addition to the brick shale which is the mainstay of the business today. For all the ups and downs of the housing market, new buildings such as factories, government offices, hospitals and other institutions continue the demand for traditional building materials.

Barrie Booth's son Matthew, a University graduate, is the fourth generation of the Booth family to join the firm. Matthew and younger sister Sarah, (a bar student at Gray's Inn, London who is training to be a Barrister), have both worked in the business over the years and offer useful qualifications to such a diverse business. Indeed, the increasing bureaucratic demands even required that a computer programme be specially produced for it.

With continuing high standards of quality, efficiency and innovation, James Booth (Bolton) Ltd will continue to offer 'Cheerful Service' into the next Millennium.

Top left: The very first rear end loader that Booths acquired in 1978. It was capable of compacting the contents of ten skips. Above: The first skip loader that the Company owned. Below: The present site owned by Booths but shared by two other companies.

The Mill on the Lake

Red Bridge Mill, situated on the borders of Bolton and Radcliffe, is home to an internationally renowned company that today straddles twin industries - paper and textiles - with a turnover in excess of £8m, a worldwide customer base, and a burgeoning product range in four main areas: stationery, security items, publishing and packaging.

The factory (as it now is) was originally built around 1750. Blessed with its own water supply in the form of a lake (or lodge), it started life as a paper mill before being bought by D Constantine & Co, and transformed into a bleaching and commission finishing business in 1860. Most of its output at that time - mainly nainsooks and dhooties - were exported to India. At the end of the century, however, India developed her own weaving and finishing industry and the mill cried out for a new role.

In 1927, James Cort identified a growing market in the area for bookbinding and tracing cloth and established the Red Bridge Book Cloth Company at the site. Much of the machinery still in use today dates from that time - uniquely engineered, and modified to serve new purposes as the years have passed, it provides a fascinating insight into the specialised world of bookcloth manufacture.

In the early days, the firm was owned jointly by James Cort and the Glaister family, who succeeded the Constantines and were to be the last mill-owners to occupy the manor house at the end of the mill drive. During World War II, the house briefly provided accommodation for Lord Montgomery of Alamein, at a time when the factory's output was given over entirely to the production of blackout material.

If the war brought its own demands and markets, the arrival of new technology, amid a culture of diversification, encouraged the firm to extend its operation in the 1970s. It's a matter of some regret to booklovers in general that the production of traditional clothbound volumes is diminishing. Drawn-on paper covers have all but superseded them in the popular retail market - and the perennial attraction, for publishers at any rate, of the modern dust jacket has had a serious impact on the market for high-quality bookbinding materials. The old skills survive - but Red Bridge was quick to recognise that other products must be developed alongside.

Experience gained in the coating of textiles augured well for a move into coated papers - which held great appeal for the world of packaging as well as

Left: James Cort who established the Red Bridge Book Cloth Company. **Top right:** *One of Red Bridge's coating machines.* **Below:** *Examples of wallpaper and fabric swatches, bound using Red Bridge coated papers.*

in 1997, and in 1998 a distributor was appointed in Beijing.

A global operation, certainly - but a company still proud of its long-serving Bolton workforce. Generations of many families have passed through its employ. Recruitment seldom requires advertisement - there remains a strong tradition of other family members joining the team when and if they can - and long service is highly valued. Denis Wolstenholme, the current Managing Director, has himself been at the firm for 35 years and in his time has probably tackled every task imaginable within the factory. Now at the helm of this multi-faceted, state-of-the-art concern he is both confident of a dynamic future full of opportunity and demonstrably proud of the 80 or so staff in a Lancashire mill - who day after day, year after year make it all possible.

Top Left: Examples of books bound with Red Bridge's covering material. Top right: Denis Wolstenholme and Hong Kong sales staff at their Second Anniversary Dinner in 1998. Below: The Biggest Book in Bradford a fine example of Red Bridge's covering material.

publishing - and the change was formalised by a new name: Red Bridge (Bolton) Ltd. In 1974, the company passed into the hands of the Whitecroft Group, based in Wilmslow, and the modern era began.

The move into coated papers marked a turning point for the company. The diversity of the product range now offered is astonishing: passport covers for 40 nationalities are currently made from Red Bridge Securalin - a high specification material developed in Bolton that withstands high temperatures, comes in a wide spectrum of colours, and is robust in its survival of the most unforgiving treatment at airports and seaports throughout the world. Stationery materials are used for the production of box files, ring binders and account books, whilst many Red Bridge products cover stylish presentation cases for jewellery, pens and watches.

Export markets first exploited in the 1960s now account for 50% of the firm's production. More than 50 countries now provide customers for Red Bridge - and the firm's two major competitors - large American corporations - are being taken on and beaten time and again for market share. In 1996 a Red Bridge office opened in Hong Kong and following another name change - to Red Bridge International - a German office opened

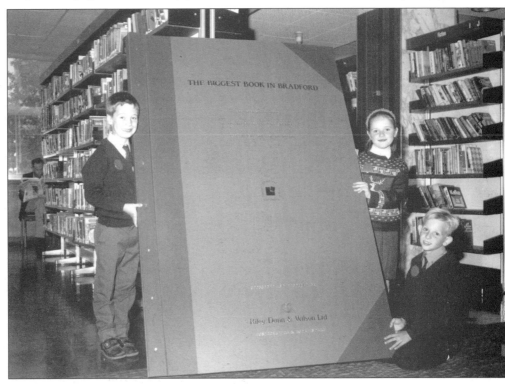

Preserving Bolton's heritage for future generations

<B>olton," The Times once said, " . . is a town that believes in moving with the times and making the most of itself." The last 20 years have indeed seen many changes in Bolton, some brought in by the motorway network which has grown up around the town and made it more accessible to people from the surrounding areas, others simply in response to the changing times. It is generally accepted that the price a town must pay for change is the sacrifice of a little piece of its history, and so each new planning application has to show that the benefits it will bring to the town outweigh any aesthetic disadvantages. Only exceptionally does an opportunity arise for a town to enjoy all the advantages of a modern development whilst still retaining it's inherent character.

There can be no better example of a development which has managed to do just this, than The Shipgates Shopping Centre, which has preserved the historic facade of one of Bolton's most magnificent buildings and created, behind the original frontage, a thriving, state-of-

the-art shopping centre which can compete with any in England.

Built in 1989 and opened in November 1990, the idea for The Gates Shopping Centres had actually started as far back as 1984. The site chosen for the project was the building on Mealhouse Lane which was then still occupied by the Bolton Evening News. This impressive, if, to some, rather austere edifice, with its ornate masonry work, was built for the Bolton Evening News in the 1870s, and subsequently became a listed building. From the inception of the scheme, it was planned that, externally, the front of this building should be the focal point of The Gates. For over a century, these walls had represented, to the people of Bolton, the source of local news coverage, and, inside, the building had been alive with

Top left: The Bolton Evening News as it looked in 1907.
Below: The same building pictured in March 1993, shortly after the signage had been changed.

attracted stores of such a high calibre is a testimony to their success. The Centre has direct wheelchair access, so, situated as it is right in the middle of town, it brings all these stores within easy reach of the disabled. There are also two stylish and affordable eating areas, where patrons can enjoy their meal sitting by the original arched Victorian windows which form part of the facade of the building.

discussion of Bolton's hopes, plans, controversies and achievements; so it seemed appropriate that the site's new lease of life should allow it to carry on its tradition of being a community building at the hub of local life.

During the building works, the external walls and the slate roof were preserved intact whilst the building was completely gutted. The new design of the interior is a tasteful blend of Victorian elegance with up-to-date technology, featuring scissor escalators and scenic lifts and creating a pleasant atmosphere for shoppers and employees alike. Shops are on two floors, and retailers include major High Street stores such as Boots, Tiny Computers, Midas Jewellers and The Phone People, Romanis of Chester, Massimo, Mediterranean Collection, Bodyactive, Streetwise Sports, The Terrace Restaurant . . . the list continues to grow. The owners and management aim to provide suitable accommodation for retailers so that they, in turn, can meet the requirements of the shopping public of the Bolton area; and the fact that the Centre has

The courage of the developers, Mantaphase (a partnership between Higgs & Hill and Arrowcroft PLC) in opening the Centre in the middle of a recession has been fully vindicated, with the current population of Bolton standing at over 250,000, and its proximity to the M6/M62 motorway network and the A6 and A58 trunk roads giving it a thirty minute catchment area of over two million people. The Centre has its own well-lit undercover car-park, so whether customers have driven a couple of miles or travelled in from other parts of the prosperous North West, they are assured of convenient parking. The Gates Shopping Centre offers everything the modern shopper could ask for; but for Bolton it is more than simply a successful commercial enterprise; it has been the means of ensuring that a part of Bolton's heritage will be preserved for future generations. The architecturally distinguished building which many people still remember as The Bolton Evening News will remain part of Bolton's heritage, playing as central a role as ever in community life.

Top left: Mr Pat Duckett, the Centre Manager, pictured during construction in 1990. Left: Visitors to the centre enjoying lunch in the Terrace Restaurant. Below: A recent view of the entrance to The Gates Shopping Centre.

A company Bolton can be proud of

The name of Prestons has long been synonymous throughout the North of England as the leading independent jewellers in the region. But the Prestons that we all know today as a business with branches in many parts of the country began over a century and a quarter ago in Bolton - when watchmaker James Preston opened for business.

The early years

1869 was the year that James Preston began selling watches and jewellery in Bolton. The town was enjoying the relative prosperity that the industrial revolution and the booming cotton trade had brought. Business prospered and the impressive premises at Deansgate in the centre of Bolton were acquired and developed in 1904. By the turn of the century, Prestons had already forced a reputation as the most comprehensive and prestigious jewellers outside London, with customers coming to Bolton from many other parts of the country, with word of mouth being the major medium for the business to attract new customers. In 1905 James Preston died, leaving Gertrude Sheppard to run the business.

Gertrude Sheppard, great aunt of the present Managing Director, Andrew Duckworth, had been working for James Preston since the age of fourteen.

By 1920, Gertrude Sheppard had acquired a controlling interest in the company and since that time Prestons has been a family run business.

Left: The use of matchbooks and train tickets for advertising isn't a new idea. These examples were produced by Prestons decades ago.
Below: The 1968 visit of Queen elizabeth to the town is captured in this photograph.

seen them open branches outside their traditional northern base. They now have outlets in York, Guildford and Windsor, and watch concession in House of Fraser store in Birmingham. In March 1994 Prestons acquired Croydons - another independent jeweller with two outlets in Bury St. Edmunds and Ipswich, and more recently Prestons opened their first outlet in Scotland, when their watch concession in Jenners department store, Edinburgh, was opened.

The 'family run feel' is strong to this day and Andrew's brother Quentin plays a key role as the Director responsible for sales and marketing. Ian Valentine is the Financial Director. A third brother, Neil, takes an interest, but, not a direct role as he has his own successful business. Looking towards the future the plan is to keep growing but at a rate which enables the company to choose the right store in the right town, and to enable their legendary levels of customer care and market knowledge to be maintained at the levels that Prestons customers have come to expect over the last century and a quarter.

Above and below: Over the years the interior layout and designs of Prestons flagship store at Bolton has changed considerably. The picture below is how the Gift department looks today, whilst the above photograph is a late 1960s view of the same floor as a silver showroom, showing how times have moved on. One thing that hasn't changed at Prestons is the impeccable standards of service, choice and value for money that Prestons offer.

The age of expansion

By the 1950s Prestons had continued to build on their reputation as the premier Jewellers outside London. This was also the point in time that Gordon Duckworth took over the reins. Realising that demand was continuing to grow, Gordon Duckworth soon began a phase of expansion which saw Prestons open a branch in Leigh, among others.

The Leigh branch was an immediate success and Prestons were able to consolidate their position throughout the 1960s, operating from more than one outlet. Gordon Duckworth's son Andrew joined Prestons in 1972 and shortly after this a new marketing tactic saw Prestons become probably first jewellery retailer in the country to advertise on television.

1970s to the present day

The decision to use the medium of television for Prestons' advertising was to be a major factor in the company's growth over the following fifteen years. The various advertising campaigns during the seventies and eighties established Prestons as "The Diamond Centre of the North - Prestons of Bolton", and this is the phrase that most people still use to describe the company.

In 1980 Andrew Duckworth became Managing Director of Prestons with Gordon Duckworth becoming Chairman. In recent years Prestons have undertaken a planned expansion that has

Bringing benefits to Bolton

The Bolton and District Hospital Saturday Fund is one of the oldest established groups in Bolton. Its origins go back almost two hundred years, and to trace its evolution it is necessary to go back to the circumstances surrounding the establishment of Bolton Infirmary.

The provision of adequate care for the sick and elderly is not a new issue; records show that in the early 19th century there was widespread public concern in the Bolton area over the lack of facilities to treat the sick. The inhabitants of Great Bolton and Little Bolton held a meeting on 1 December 1813, at which it was decided that "a public dispensary be instituted". This "public dispensary" came into being on 7 June 1814, and was known as The Bolton Dispensary. Initially it was housed in one small cottage in Mawdsley Street. Its official purpose was for "the relief of the sick and poor in this town and neighbourhood and for the benefit of those who are not able to purchase advice and medicine for themselves". Clearly the people of Bolton had been right in asserting that there was a need for such an institution; after only six months it became necessary to take over an adjoining cottage, and during the first year it provided treatment to 1,152 patients. In 1827 a new Dispensary with seven beds was opened in Nelson Square, at a cost of some £1700; by 1838 many extensions had been added and 40 in-patients could be accommodated. The extensions were officially opened on the coronation day of Queen Victoria, 28 June 1838. By 1876 it was generally acknowledged that what Bolton really needed was an Infirmary, and it was estimated that "not less than £70,000 will be required to provide it and partially endow it". A Committee was set up in 1877 with the specific objective of raising money for this purpose. The tremendous sum of £1,300 was raised during the first year, and this achievement is a great tribute to the untiring efforts of the fundraisers and the generosity of the people of Bolton. One very effective method of collection which the Committee employed was having collectors stand at the Mill gates each Saturday morning to collect 1d from every mill worker as they came out. It was from this custom that the Committee got the unofficial title of 'Hospital Saturday', and it officially adopted this as its name in 1881.

The new Infirmary was opened on 21 July 1883 by Alderman Joseph Musgrave JP, and it is reported that, as part of the opening ceremony, the Hospital Saturday Committee organised a grand parade through the town, with all the trades and friendly societies represented, thus beginning an annual tradition which is believed to have been observed until the Second World War.

Once the Infirmary had been built and equipped, the Hospital Saturday Committee had technically

A Family Tradition

JAMES BRISCOE *Secretary* 1877–1915

A E BRISCOE *Secretary* 1915–1936

J N BRISCOE *Secretary* 1953–1973

Top right: A fund collector in 1927. Centre: Members of the Briscoe family who all took on the role of secretary for the fund, from left to right: James Briscoe, A E Briscoe and J N Briscoe. Left: The final presentation of Hospital Saturday Income to officials at Bolton Royal Infirmary in July 1948, prior to the hospital becoming part of the National Health Service.

stopped, their involvement with the health needs of the people of Bolton has continued. They still support the local NHS Hospitals by donating medical equipment and by organising fund-raising events to pay for patient amenities over and above those provided by the NHS. They also provide a Health Care Cash Plan for their members. Many local and National companies arrange membership for their employees and deduct the contribution, currently from an incredible seventy-five pence per week, via the payroll. Members are entitled to claim money towards the cost of eye care and dental treatment and the cost of surgical appliances. They also receive a sum of money for each night they spend as an in-patient. In addition there are also Maternity grants, assistance with Physiotherapist's or Specialist's fees, Prescription Charges and free benefits for dependant children.

Over the years, the Hospital Saturday Fund's tireless commitment to its objectives has helped countless local people at times of need. Bolton counts itself fortunate to have such an institution, and we all hope that it continues for many years to come.

fulfilled its original purpose. However, it had proved so successful in raising and controlling funds that it was agreed that it should continue to fund and manage the Infirmary, and this it did until 1948, when the National Health Service was introduced and the running of hospitals was taken over by the Government.

But by that time Hospital Saturday had become an invaluable part of Bolton's heritage, and it was unthinkable that institution which had been of such benefit to the community in the past should be disbanded. So, although Hospital Saturday's official responsibility for the management of the Infirmary

Above: Coronation House, 16 Silverwell Street, Bolton. *The head office of the Saturday Fund, pictured in 1954.*
Below: *Bolton Royal Infirmary, pictured in 1965.*

The Company from Bolton that keeps the world turning

Most people's eyes will have been caught, at one time or anothet, by a moving display in a shop window or at an exhibition ... and almost certainly the design and technology behind that movement will have been developed by what must be one of Bolton's most innovative companies, British Turntable.

These days moving displays are often used to attract customers' attention, but, in the 1950s, when John Entwistle - a well known Bolton businessman - wanted a turntable to use permanently in the showroom of his motor dealership, Entwistle Walker, he could not find anybody to supply one.

Mr Entwistle's son, also named John, was at that time a trainee Management Accountant with De Havilland Company. He began thinking about the gap in the market which his father had uncovered, and, in 1959, set up Bolton Turntable Company in a room in Flash Street Mill, now demolished with the Town Centre's Sainsbury store standing on the old site.

From these premises the company's first vehicle turntable was designed, produced and marketed. This turntable, the Merlin 'S', has been supplied in quantity to over 100 countries and is now used by most of the world's motor manufacturers.

John Entwistle Junior's timing in establishing Bolton Turntable Co could hardly have been better. With the 60s came the explosion of the fashion scene, with Carnaby Street and the King's Road, Chelsea at its heart. Many new boutiques sprang up, and revolving displays were just what they needed. One of them, Stop the Shop on the King's Road, in fact was a turntable - shoppers literally stepped onto a moving floor direct from the road.

During the 60s Bolton Turntable Co supplied the turntables for many impressive displays, including the multi-level revolving display which was to be the central feature of the open well at the entrance to the new Miss Selfridge in Kensington's Brompton Road.

Having firmly established itself in two major markets - motor manufacturing and High Street retailing - Bolton Turntable, now British Turntable Co Ltd to reflect its international standing, grew rapidly. Only three years after taking the small room in Flash Street Mill the company had moved into purpose-built premises, moving again within 10 years to its present Head Office buildings on Emblem Street.

Above: Part of the showroom display at Bristol Street Motors in Birmingham in the late 1960s.
Left: The revolving display at Miss Selfridge.

The company's Merlin range of vehicle turntables, which now includes the Merlin 'S', Merlin Major and Merlin Olympian models, is in demand throughout the world for their reliability and cost-effectiveness for showrooms, motor shows and exhibitions. In the retail industry a huge and diverse range of turntables is available for general display and point-of-purchase use, arything, in fact, from compact units for displaying small items such as watches and jewellery to large carousels and even eye-catching ceiling-suspended units. And they don't have to rotate - units can be designed to tilt and undulate to create striking effects.

But there's much more to this diverse and innovative company. British Tuntable's technology and design has extended far beyond its two original markets, which are nevertheless still major areas of growth for the company as continuous product development uncovers new spheres of operation.

An Industrial Division was formed to provide specialised revolves for non-destructive and ultra-sonic testing, where anything from a mobile phone to a large tank or aircraft needs to be rotated for electro-magnetic compatability (EMC) testing. In city centre and commercial developments the use of a turntable can reduce the amount of room needed for manoeuvring delivery vehicles and cars, enabling space to be used

more effectively. Some recent projects even include revolving restaurants and Turntable Divisible Auditoriums (TDAS) such as those installed in the Edinburgh International Conference Centre.

A flourishing Hire Division provides a range of revolves for use in the exhibitions industry - anyone visiting a major Motor Show will have seen more than just a few turntables from British Turntable in action. The film, TV and video industries constantly call on British Turntable to provide movement for special effects, whether it be for a fashion catwalk show, a major block-busting movie, a game show or high drama. A special range of revolving stages has been developed to meet the needs of this growth industry. And anyone who has visited Blackpool during the Autumn illuminations may have noticed the rotating figurines, clocks and ornaments which came to life on British Turntable revolves.

Selling into niche markets in over 120 countries, British Turntable is justifiably proud of the large amount of repeat orders which it receives, and of the fact that most of its new business is gained from recommendations from satisfied customers. From the beginning it has ensured that its products are designed and engineered to stringent quality standards, and its programme of continuous research and development means that no opportunity is lost In using advances in technology to improve its existing products and extend its range. Its success is no doubt due to these factors and also to others; the astuteness of John Entwistle, its founder and current Chairman, in rising to the challenge of filling the gap in the market which was revealed when his father wanted to be able to revolve the cars in this showroom; and in the company's uncanny knack of recruiting personnel with complementary skills, combining age and experience with a new breed of young graduates all dedicated to growing the company worldwide from its Bolton home.

Above: A vehicle turntable improves delivery access in the centre of historic Chester.
Left: A revolving display for Blackpool illuminations.

Top of the League - at home and abroad

In 1919 Mr Hallet, a coal merchant, and Mr Broughton, proprietor of J J Broughton sports shop in Wigan, despaired of finding rugby jerseys of the quality they wanted, and so they founded a company to make their own. The company was named Halbro after its two founders, and the very first Halbro rugby jerseys ever made were produced in a stable in Wigan.

In the same year, a few miles down the road in Horwich, Walter Moores established a weaving company, Moreton Mill. Whilst Halbro were establishing themselves in Wigan as innovators in rugby clothing design and quality, Moreton Mill was also prospering under the guidance of Walter Moores; he was later joined by his two sons, Jack and Bert, and they acquired another mill in Turton in 1935, running a total of 1,000 Lancashire looms. Unfortunately the decline in the Lancashire textiles industry in the 1950s brought an end to the company's success; it was the government's policy to combat overproduction by shrinking the industry, and mills were given incentives to break up their machinery and cease trading. The Moores family business closed its doors in 1959.

Above: A 1931c catalogue of the company's products.
Right: The Wigan factory in the early 1930s.

The closure of Moreton Mills left Walter, Jack and Bert in a position to buy another business, and it was suggested to them by Cyril Holmes, Bolton's Olympic runner and International rugby player, that there was a small sportswear company in Wigan which might be a good investment. The company in question was, of course, Halbro, which was still in the hands of the Hallet family although by that time none of them were actively involved in the business. Mr Hallet had bought out Mr Broughton in 1924, and when he died in 1950 he left the company to his five daughters. Small though it was, Halbro had some good accounts, including the school outfitting division of Harrod's, and Walter, Jack and Bert Moores decided to buy.

With Walter starting to take a back seat, Bert and Jack developed the company and in 1965 moved it into their existing weaving mill in Horwich, which gave them more room to expand. Throughout its history the company has never lost sight of its original goal, the production of strong, high quality rugby clothing, specially designed to withstand the punishment it has to undergo during a game of professional rugby. Halbro knits its own fabric in its very versatile knitting plant of 45 machines including very modern multi-feed machines and quick pattern change machines; it produces the garments; and it has its own plant of embroidery

worldwide, as well as retailers specialising in rugby from all rugby playing nations - Fiji, Japan, Malaysia, USA, Canada, all Europe, the Middle East, Hong Kong and many more. In 1986 another factory was opened in Wigan to produce rugby shorts. Expansion continued, and in 1995 the factory moved across the road into a larger part of the Moreton Mill building which provided accommodation of 55,000 square feet all on one floor. This gave it room to move the machines from the Wigan factory into Horwich. The Wigan factory was closed, but the company runs a bus from Wigan each day for their employees.

Another consequence of the move was that Halbro has been able to completely renovate the old mill , thus making a tremendous improvement to the appearance of the area of Horwich near the Crown Hotel.

With the next generation of Moores now involved in the business - Jack's son Robert joined the company in 1971 and Bert's son John in 1984 - the family's success story is set to continue into the next millennium.

Above: Halbro made all the kit used in the TV programme 'First Kangaroos', about the first Aussie touring side, starring Dennis Waterman.
Left: A recent promotional photograph.
Below: The company's premises today.

machines to badge the jerseys. 100% cotton garments are still produced, but these days acrylic and polyester fibres are also used, and customers can choose from a wide range of weights and fabrics. Halbro also offers, uniquely, a bespoke tailoring service, and will custom make as few as twelve garments to a customer's specific design.

By the 1980s Halbro had become well established as an international competitor, exporting to over 30 countries, and the 1990s have seen Halbro firmly established as the largest rugbywear manufacturer in the world. Its current UK market includes retail sports shops, school outfitters, rugby clubs, major sport companies such as Reebok and Nike, and customers in the corporate sector including Famous Grouse and Glen Turret, and with a partner factory in Providence, Rhode Island, USA manufacturing rugby clothing, and a licensing agreement in Japan, it supplies over 2,000 rugby clubs

An early 1960s view of Churchgate looking towards the tall tower of the Parish Church.

ACKNOWLEDGMENTS

THE PUBLISHERS WOULD LIKE TO THANK

BOLTON ARCHIVES & LOCAL STUDIES

BOLTON EVENING NEWS

CHRIS DRIVER

Bolton Archives and Bolton Museum are keen to add to their collections of photographs of Bolton and district. If you have any interesting local photographs or postcards which you would consider donating, selling or lending to them, please contact Barry Mills (Tel Bolton 522311 ext 2179) or John McGoldrick (Tel Bolton 522311 ext 2213).

You are welcome to see their collection of local photographs, maps, books, newspapers, archives and family history sources in the Archives & Local Studies Searchroom at Bolton Central Library, Le Mans Crescent, Bolton BL1 1SE.